Collector's Guide to

QUARTZ

and Other Silica Minerals

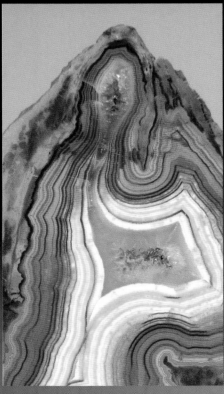

Schiffer Earth Science Monographs Volume 13

Schiffer Publishing Ltd

4880 Lower Valley Road • Atglen, PA 19310

Robert J. Lauf

Other Schiffer Books By The Author:
Collector's Guide to the Axinite Group. ISBN: 9780764332166. $19.99.
Collector's Guide to the Epidote Group. ISBN: 9780764330483. $19.99.
Collector's Guide to the Garnet Group. ISBN: 9780076434003 1. $19.99.
Collector's Guide to Silicate Crystal Structures. ISBN: 9780764335792.
    $19.99.
Collector's Guide to the Tourmaline Group. ISBN: 9780764337758.
    $19.99.
Collector's Guide to the Vesuvianite Group. ISBN: 9780764332159.
    $19.99.

Other Schiffer Books on Related Subjects:
Collector's Guide to Fluorite. Arvid Eric Pasto. ISBN: 9780764331930.
    Price: $19.99.

Designed by Mark David Bowyer
Type set in Arno Pro / Humanist 521 BT

ISBN: 978-0-7643-4161-8
Printed in China

Schiffer Books are available at special discounts for bulk purchases for sales promotions or premiums. Special editions, including personalized covers, corporate imprints, and excerpts can be created in large quantities for special needs. For more information contact the publisher:

Published by Schiffer Publishing Ltd.
4880 Lower Valley Road
Atglen, PA 19310
Phone: (610) 593-1777; Fax: (610) 593-2002
E-mail: Info@schifferbooks.com

For the largest selection of fine reference
books on this and related subjects,
please visit our website at **www.schifferbooks.com**
We are always looking for people to write books
on new and related subjects.
If you have an idea for a book, please contact us at
proposals@schifferbooks.com

This book may be purchased from the publisher.
Include $5.00 for shipping.
Please try your bookstore first.
You may write for a free catalog.

In Europe, Schiffer books are distributed by
Bushwood Books
6 Marksbury Ave.
Kew Gardens
Surrey TW9 4JF England
Phone: 44 (0) 20 8392 8585; Fax: 44 (0) 20 8392 9876
E-mail: info@bushwoodbooks.co.uk
Website: www.bushwoodbooks.co.uk

Contents

Preface

This volume continues a series of monographs on important groups of so-called rock forming silicates, the purpose of which is to help mineral collectors gain a better appreciation of these complex minerals. Because of the importance of rock forming minerals in geological processes, they are the subject of extensive published research, much of which has been brought together in the five-volume compendium *Rock-Forming Minerals* by Deer, Howie, and Zussman, first published in 1962, and the greatly expanded Second Edition thereof. Among rock-forming minerals, quartz is a favorite of mineral collectors because it readily forms sharp crystals, which can be large and water-clear, in a wide range of colors, from colorless to pink, purple, yellow, and brown. Quartz crystals may be associated with many other species and often contain striking inclusions of colorful minerals as well as fluids and gas bubbles. For the specialty collector, quartz provides fine examples of twins and pseudomorphs, and quartz or opal is the mineralizing agent responsible for most fossils and petrified wood.

Quartz is widespread throughout the world and represents about 12% of the earth's crust. Thus, it is of great importance to the geologist and geochemist because so many mineral-forming reactions involve quartz. The mineralogy of "pure" crystalline silica, SiO_2, is surprisingly complicated, occupying an entire volume of the 7th Edition of *The System of Mineralogy* (Frondel 1962). A number of polymorphs exist, several of which are formed at high pressures and only exist metastably under ordinary conditions. In addition to the polymorphs of silica, this volume will treat several other minerals and mineraloids of interest, including: lechatelierite, which is a natural glass found particularly in fulgurites; opal, which is a hydrous form of colloidal silica; and two natural clathrates, chibaite and melanophlogite.

The book is organized as follows: After a brief introduction, the general treatment begins with an explanation of the chemistry and taxonomy of the silica polymorphs. A section on their formation and geochemistry explains the kinds of environments where silica minerals are formed. Then, an entry for each mineral provides locality information and full-color photos wherever possible so that collectors can see what good specimens look like and which minerals one might expect to find in association with them. An extensive bibliography is provided for readers who wish to learn more about particular topics.

Acknowledgments

The following colleagues kindly provided technical information, literature, and helpful discussions: Ahmed El Goresy, *Universität Bayreuth, Germany*; Gary Maddox, *Apalachee Minerals*; Arvid Pasto. Important specimens and background information were supplied by: John Betts; Dave Bunk; Sharon Cisneros, *Mineralogical Research Co.*; Richard Dale, *Dale Minerals*; Luis De Los Santos, *St. Paul Gems and Minerals*; Beau Gordon, *Jendon Minerals*; Shields Flynn, *Trafford-Flynn Minerals*; Pete Heckscher, *The Crystal Circle*; Leonard Himes, *Minerals America*; David Lare, *Jeffrey Mining*; Tony Nikischer, *Excalibur Mineral Co.*; Alfredo Petrov; Neal Pfaff, *M. Phantom Minerals*; Jeff Schlottman, *Crystal Perfection*; Jaye Smith, *The Rocksmiths*; Brian Stefanec, *Universal Rock Shop*; Sergey Vasiliev, *Systematic Mineralogy*; Chris Wright, *Wright's Rock Shop*.

Introduction

Quartz is ubiquitous in the environment and makes up roughly 12% of the earth's crust; it is the most common mineral after all the feldspars taken together as a *group*. Thus, it is of great importance to the geologist and geochemist because so many mineral-forming reactions involve quartz.

Quartz is a favorite of mineral collectors because sharp, colorful crystal specimens, even fairly large ones, are relatively plentiful and inexpensive. Quartz crystals may be associated with many other species and often contain striking inclusions of colorful minerals as well as fluids and gas bubbles. Quartz, agate, and opal are important in the gem and lapidary trades, and quartz is a major industrial material with vast quantities mined or dredged for sand and other construction materials.

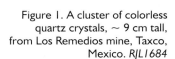

Figure 1. A cluster of colorless quartz crystals, ~ 9 cm tall, from Los Remedios mine, Taxco, Mexico. *RJL1684*

Most minerals in the group are not intrinsically fluorescent; however, opal is often fluorescent green in short wave or long wave ultraviolet light (SWUV, LWUV) because of microscopic inclusions of uranium compounds or the presence of uranyl ions that have been adsorbed onto the surfaces of the colloidal particles that make up the opal structure. Similar fluorescence can be seen in many agates.

Figure 2. Colorless, transparent hyalite opal from Square Top Mountain, Queensland, Australia, forming a bubbly mass ~2 cm wide on matrix. *RJL3869*

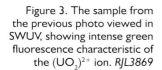 Figure 3. The sample from the previous photo viewed in SWUV, showing intense green fluorescence characteristic of the $(UO_2)^{2+}$ ion. *RJL3869*

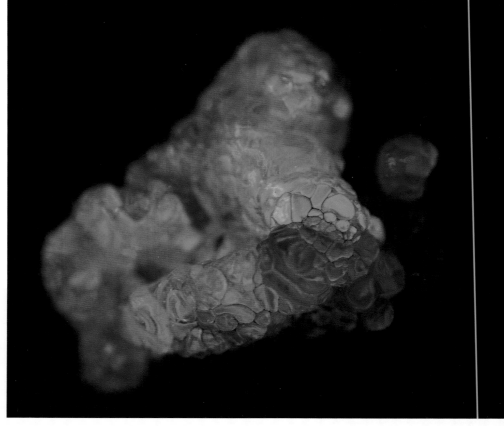

Gemology

The sheer quantity of gem and lapidary materials that involve quartz or other silica-based material, such as petrified wood, dwarfs the production of most other gemstones. Hurlbut and Switzer (1979) state that, "Of all the minerals used as gems none compares with quartz in its diversity of occurrence and in abundance of varieties." They divide gem quartz into two groups:

Coarsely crystalline varieties, including rock crystal (colorless), citrine (yellow to orange), amethyst (purple), smoky (brown to black), rose (pink), and quartz with inclusions (rutilated quartz, tourmalinated quartz, aventurine, and tiger's eye).

Microcrystalline varieties, including various forms of chalcedony, such as agate, carnelian, chrysoprase, sard, moss agate, and onyx, as well as granular types such as jasper.

Opal is produced in significantly lower quantities than quartz or chalcedony, but in the case of precious opal, the material is far more valuable on a per-carat basis.

Figure 4. Some cut stones illustrating the range of lapidary materials based on silica minerals: (top row, left to right) opalized wood, tumbled green aventurine, red agate, (bottom row, left to right) amethyst, precious opal, and smoky quartz.

Industrial uses

Silica is a major industrial commodity that encompasses many different products and applications, including industrial sand and gravel, quartz crystal, special silica stone products, and tripoli (Dolley 2011):

Industrial sand and gravel includes sands and gravels with high SiO_2 content; applications include abrasives, filtration media, foundry molds, golf course and recreational sand, hydraulic fracturing proppants, and raw materials for glassmaking and silicon production. Mining is normally done by open pit or dredging, with annual production of ~25-30M metric tons and a value of $800-900M (~$30/metric ton).

Electronic-grade quartz crystal has been mostly produced synthetically since about 1971, using mined quartz, primarily from Brazil and Madagascar, as a feedstock. About *ten billion* quartz crystal oscillators are manufactured worldwide each year.

Silica stone products, made from novaculite, quartzite, and other microcrystalline silica rocks, are used for abrasive tools such as deburring media, grinding pebbles, grindstones, hones, oilstones, etc.

Tripoli includes extremely fine-grained silica (typically 1-10 μm particles, with some much smaller) with 1-2% of clay or iron oxide. It has unique abrasive properties because the individual grains are hard, but they have a smooth, rounded shape, yielding a very mild abrasive used in such things as toothpaste, polishing compounds, and buffing compounds for automobile finishing. Tripoli is also used as a filler in paints, rubber and plastic products, brake friction compounds, and caulking compounds.

Taxonomy of the Silica Minerals

The mineralogy of "pure" crystalline silica, SiO_2, is surprisingly complicated, occupying an entire volume of the 7th Edition of *The System of Mineralogy* (Frondel 1962). A number of polymorphs exist, several of which are formed at high pressures and only exist metastably under ordinary conditions. The high pressure polymorphs coesite, stishovite, and seifertite have all been found in nature and are thus valid mineral species; another high-pressure silica polymorph, *keatite*, is only known as a synthetic phase as of this writing and will not be covered here. In addition, this book will treat several other minerals and mineraloids of interest, viz., lechatelierite, which is a natural silica glass found particularly in fulgurites, opal, a hydrous form of colloidal silica, and two natural clathrates, chibaite and melanophlogite (Momma et al. 2011).

In a classic paper on silica minerals, Rogers (1928) remarked, "It seems probable that all the forms of silica capable of existing at atmospheric pressures are now known. But it is not safe to say that all the possible distinct forms of silica are known, for polymorphism is a general phenomenon of nature and there is no theoretical limit to the number of polymorphous modifications of any chemical substance." This observation holds true today, as new forms of silica continue to be described.

Table 1.
The silica minerals

Mineral	Formula	Symmetry	Stable Range[a], °C
α-Quartz	SiO_2	trigonal	< 573
β-Quartz	SiO_2	hexagonal	573-870
α-Tridymite	SiO_2	orthorhombic	<117 (metastable)
β-Tridymite	SiO_2	hexagonal	870-1470
α-Cristobalite	SiO_2	tetragonal	<200 (metastable)
β-Cristobalite	SiO_2	isometric	1475-1713
Mogánite	SiO_2	monoclinic	
Coesite[b]	SiO_2	monoclinic	metastable
Stishovite[b]	SiO_2	tetragonal	metastable
Seifertite[b]	SiO_2	orthorhombic	metastable
Lechatelierite	SiO_2	amorphous	
Opal	$SiO_2 \cdot nH_2O$	amorphous[c]	
Chibaite[d,e]	$SiO_2 \cdot n(CH_4, C_2H_6, C_3H_8, C_4H_{10})$	cubic	
Melanophlogite[d]	$46SiO_2 \cdot 6(N_2, CO_2) \cdot 2(CH_4, N_2)$	cubic	

[a]Thermal stability range at atmospheric pressure (data from Deer, Howie, and Zussman 1992)

[b]Stable at high pressures

[c]The structure of opal on a fine scale is described in more detail in the text

[d]Chibaite and melanophlogite are natural clathrates

[e]$n \leq 3/17$

Crystal structure and morphology

This section will cover only the crystal structures of the SiO_2 polymorphs. The structural details of lechatelierite, melanophlogite, opal, and chibaite will be discussed in their entries in the Minerals section.

Quartz

The crystal structure of quartz is unusual in that it contains a helical arrangement of SiO_4 tetrahedra, and the helices may be either right- or left-handed. This creates the possibility of two "enantiomorphic" forms that are mirror images of one another but cannot be superposed.

Right- and left-handed quartz crystals are about equally prevalent in nature on a global basis (Frondel 1962), but careful statistical analysis has shown that one or the other may be slightly more prevalent at a particular locality (Tamara and Preston 2009). Heaney (1994) describes the confusion that has arisen over the years because different researchers have used different conventions for the settings of the unit cell. He also notes that it had been known since the early 1800s that quartz crystals of different handedness will rotate the vibration plane of polarized light in opposite senses, but it was only in the late 1950s that the handedness of a tetrahedral spiral could be associated with a particular light rotation.

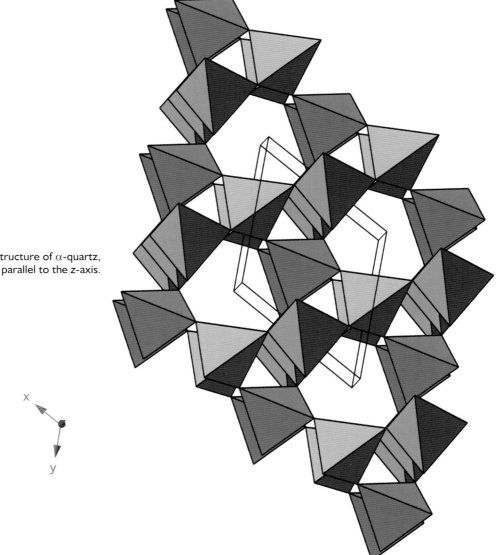

Figure 5. Crystal structure of α-quartz, viewed nearly parallel to the z-axis.

Figure 6. A portion of the structure of α-quartz (right-hand enantiomorph is shown), drawn to emphasize the arrangement of SiO$_4$ tetrahedra into right-handed helices.

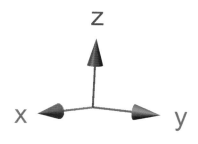

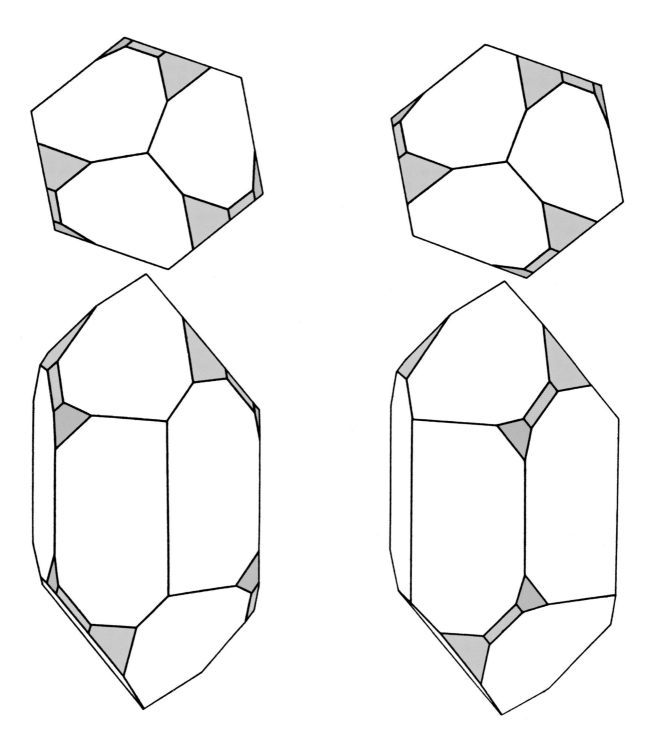

Figure 7. Comparison of quartz enantiomorphs (right-handed crystal is on the right). The relative positions of the minor forms x (green), s (blue), and z (pink) determines the "hand" of the crystal. One of the best ways to find sharp examples of right- and left-handed quartz crystals is by closely examining a group of doubly-terminated "Herkimer diamonds."

Quartz is one of the most commonly-collected minerals because of the wide range of habits and morphologies that it can display. Goldschmidt (1922) presented over 800 drawings of natural quartz crystals, with many detailed examples of both commonly seen and unusual habits, along with twins, twisted or "gwindel" crystals, and various types of surface features.

Twinning in quartz is especially important because it affects the piezoelectric behavior and renders a lot of natural raw material unsuitable for use in quartz crystal oscillators (Frondel 1945). To get an appreciation of the problem, Frondel (1962) estimated that during the wartime years of 1939-45, about twenty-five million pounds of quartz crystals were exported from Brazil, and the U.S. manufactured over eighty million oscillator plates at a cost of about a half-billion dollars. Now, of course, the industry relies on synthetically grown quartz for this purpose.

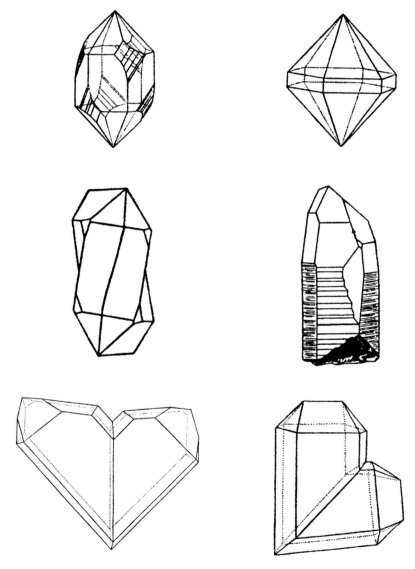

Figure 8. Drawings of natural quartz crystals, modified from Goldschmidt (1922), showing a number of less common forms.

Gault (1949) showed that twinned quartz crystals are more common than untwinned and that the frequencies of twin types and their ratios vary from one locality to another. According to Frondel (1962), "Twinning is the rule rather than the exception in quartz. Des Cloizeaux said that an untwinned quartz crystal was one of the greatest rarities of the mineral kingdom. Almost every crystal contains penetration twinning on one of the parallel-axis laws, and usually several of these laws are present simultaneously." Quartz twins can be grouped into two categories, viz., parallel-axis twins, which are usually penetration twins, and inclined-axis twins, which are usually contact twins.

Parallel-axis twins include Brazil, Dauphiné, and Combined Laws. In Dauphiné twinning, which is the most common, the twinned parts have the same "hand" and are related geometrically as by rotation of 180° around the z-axis. Brazil twins are related by reflection over $\{11\bar{2}0\}$ and are of opposite hands. Brazil twinning rarely occurs by itself, except in amethyst, but rather is usually accompanied by Dauphiné twinning. In Combined twins, the two parts are related by a combination of 180° rotation about the z-axis and a reflection over $\{11\bar{2}0\}$, or simply a reflection over $\{0001\}$. The crystal axes are parallel, but in contrast to Brazil and Dauphiné twins, the electrical polarity of the x-axes isn't reversed.

Figure 9. Quartz specimen about 5 cm tall from Beaverhead Co., Montana, illustrating a sharp "scepter" habit in which an enlarged termination grows on an existing thinner crystal shaft. *RJL1543*

Figure 10. A group of bipyramidal quartz crystals from Dal'negorsk, Russia, about 10 cm tall, colored green by microscopic inclusions. This material is sometimes mistakenly labeled "β-quartz," but it is simply an uncommon habit of α-quartz. The black crystals are ilvaite. *RJL2375*

Inclined-axis twins include four related kinds of twins that are collectively called Japan Law, as well as several rarer forms such as the Zinnwald and Zwickau Laws. All Japan Law twins are contact twins of two crystals whose z-axes are inclined at 84°33' to one another. The different subtypes are determined by whether the two individuals are of the same or opposite hand, and by the relation of the polarities of the x-axes. Many Japan twins grow in a flattened shape to create a generally tabular appearance.

Figure 12. Colorless quartz crystals with multi-faceted terminations caused by Dauphine-law twinning. The specimen, from the Chia mine, Sao Jose da Safira, Minas Gerais, Brazil, is ~7 cm tall. *RJL4156*

Figure 11. An example of "faden" quartz, in which a white line runs through the center of the crystal. This feature is attributed to some unique aspect of the growth process, but the exact mechanism remains conjectural. The main crystal group is about 5 cm tall, and there are numerous smaller faden crystals scattered across the matrix plate. The sample is from Waziristan, Pakistan. *RJL2536*

The presence of iron seems to promote the formation of Brazil-law twinning, explaining why such twinning is common in natural amethyst. McLaren and Pitkethly (1982) showed that synthetic quartz grown on twinned amethyst seeds contained new areas of twinning when iron was added to the system. Koivula and Fritsch (1989) studied this issue in detail and warned that one cannot assume that, "a twinned crystal is almost certainly of natural origin," as had been proposed by Nassau (1980).

The issue of cleavage in quartz is an interesting one. Field guides often describe quartz as having a conchoidal fracture, rather than an obvious cleavage, and this is generally true for a quartz crystal subjected to a simple hammer blow. However, Frondel (1962) clearly showed that cleavage cracks can be induced, either by thermal shock or by special methods such as the use of a carefully oriented chisel edge on a thin slice that has been cut perpendicular to the cleavage to be tested. He also notes that, "Rhombohedral cleavage surfaces 2-9 ft. across have been observed in anhedral crystals in the cores of pegmatites in western Arizona and southern California. ... It is sometimes described as a parting, and this description is more apt when, as is often the case, the crystal tends to separate into relatively thick plates which are further cleavable only with difficulty." Bloss and Gibbs (1963) applied statistical analysis to the fractures seen in crushed quartz grains and noted that the most commonly seen cleavage directions are those which break the least number of Si-O bonds. They also suggest that, "The conchoidal fracture of quartz is, to a degree, structurally controlled. The curved surfaces may represent submicroscopic combinations of cleavage planes ξ, z, r, c, s, x, m, and a."

Figure 13. A sharp example of a quartz "Japan law" twin, about 6 cm tall, from Ica, Peru. *RJL2407*

Tridymite

Heaney (1994) describes the complexity of tridymite and the inherent difficulties in studying a mineral that almost always forms very tiny crystals that contain growth twins. Furthermore, tridymite exhibits a number of structural modifications, some of which are stable over very narrow temperature ranges. Different workers have used different terminologies to identify these structural variants; in the notation introduced by Nukui, Nakazawa, and Akao (1978), the first letter signifies the crystal system of the polymorph and the second letter indicates the unit cell type. Most of these modifications, such as HP, OC, OS, MC, etc., don't normally exist at room temperature and thus are mainly of scientific interest. For the collector, the situation may be simplified as follows. Tridymite has high- and low-temperature forms; β-tridymite is stable from 870 to 1470°C, whereas α-tridymite can exist from ambient temperatures up to 117°C, but isn't the stable form of silica in that range. Ideal β-tridymite is hexagonal and the structure can best be visualized as being formed by the linkage of sheets that lie parallel to (0001). The bases of all the tetrahedra lie in the (0001) plane, but their apices point alternately in the +z and −z directions. α-Tridymite is orthorhombic; however, its structure represents only a slight deviation from that of the high-temperature form (Deer, Howie, and Zussman 1992). Tridymite generally forms small colorless tabular crystals.

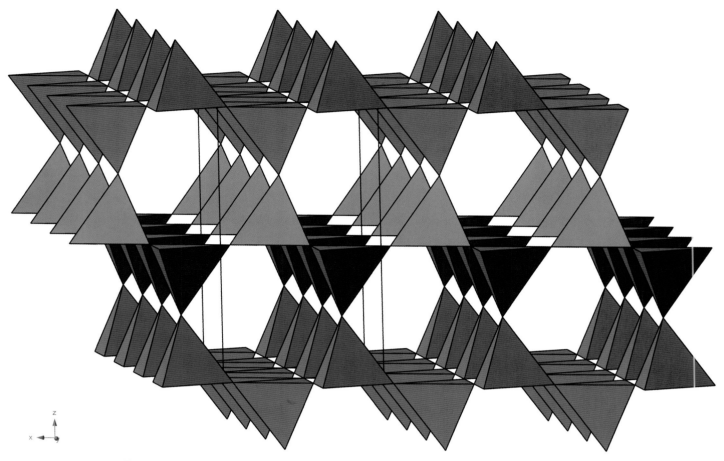

Figure 14. The structure of β-tridymite viewed normal to the z-axis.

Figure 15. SEM photo of a small tridymite crystal about 70 μm long, on acicular cassiterite, from the Thomas Range, Juab Co., Utah. *RJL1108*

Cristobalite

The structure of β-cristobalite is somewhat analogous to that of tridymite, in that it is based on sheets formed of six-membered silicate rings. But in this case, the basal oxygens of each tetrahedron, rather than being superimposed, are instead rotated 60° relative to those of the tetrahedron below it. The overall symmetry is cubic. Dollase (1965) refined the structure of α-cristobalite and showed it to be tetragonal. Cristobalite generally forms microscopic crystals (the "snow" in snowflake obsidian, for instance).

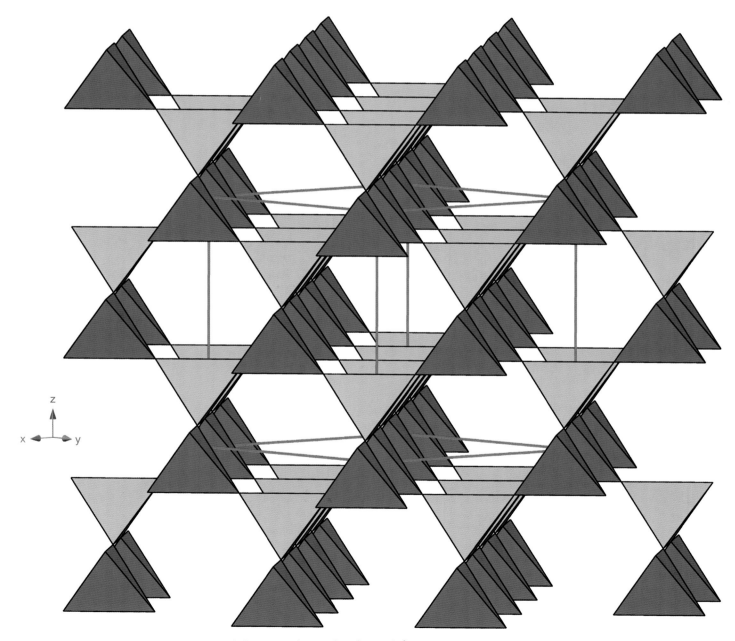

Figure 16. The structure of β-cristobalite, viewed normal to the z-axis for comparison to the structure of tridymite. The cubic unit cell is shown in red.

Mogánite

The structure of mogánite can be pictured as quartz that is Brazil twinned along (101) at the unit-cell scale, so that right-handed slabs of quartz regularly alternate with left-handed slabs, thereby generating a new, monoclinic structure. X-ray structural analysis of natural mogánite is inherently difficult because no crystals large enough for single-crystal XRD study have been found, and no one has found a way to make the material synthetically. Nevertheless, Heaney and Post (2001), using synchrotron X-ray powder diffraction, found that mogánite has high- and low-temperature forms with a phase transition around 570 K.

Figure 17. Structure of mogánite viewed almost normal to the z-axis; data from Heaney and Post (2001).

Coesite

The structure of coesite was determined by Ramsdell (1955) using synthetic material; at that time the phase had not yet been found in nature. The structure is monoclinic (pseudohexagonal), characterized by four-tetrahedron rings that are linked into a three-dimensional network that is more akin to the framework of feldspars than to the other silicate phases (Gibbs, Prewitt, and Baldwin 1977). Araki and Zoltai (1969) performed a crystal structure refinement on some of Coes's original material and noted that after fifteen years at normal pressure, the structure had not broken down, although the diffraction spots appeared to be more diffuse compared to those taken in 1959.

Stishovite

The higher-pressure polymorph, stishovite, is unusual in that the Si atoms are octahedrally coordinated, rather than tetrahedrally coordinated, so that stishovite doesn't have a classic "silicate" structure at all, but instead has essentially the same structure as rutile, with Si replacing the Ti inside coordination octahedra. Six-fold coordination allows the oxygens to pack together more efficiently, even though the individual Si-O bonds are longer than in quartz, so the stishovite structure is about 64% denser than that of coesite (Hemley, Prewitt, and Kingma 1994). The overall symmetry is tetragonal.

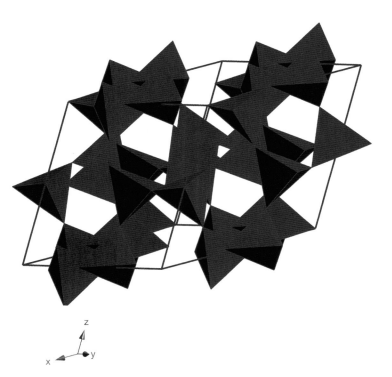

Figure 18. The monoclinic crystal structure of coesite, showing how the silicate tetrahedra are linked into a feldspar-like network; data from Araki and Zoltai (1969).

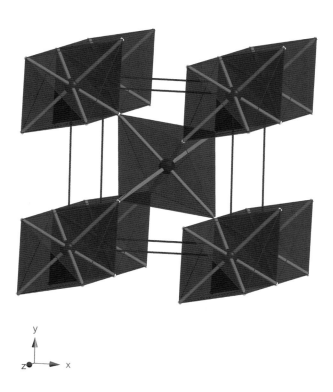

Figure 19. The crystal structure of stishovite, viewed just off the z-axis, showing the coordination octahedra, each of which has a Si at its center. To emphasize the octahedral coordination, the Si-O bonds are also shown; data from Ross et al. (1990).

Seifertite

The highest-pressure polymorph, seifertite, is stable at pressures >780 kbar and has the orthorhombic α-PbO$_2$ type structure. This structure, like that of stishovite, contains Si in distorted SiO$_6$ octahedra rather than in SiO$_4$ tetrahedra typical of normal silicate minerals. The SiO$_6$ octahedra in seifertite form kinked chains.

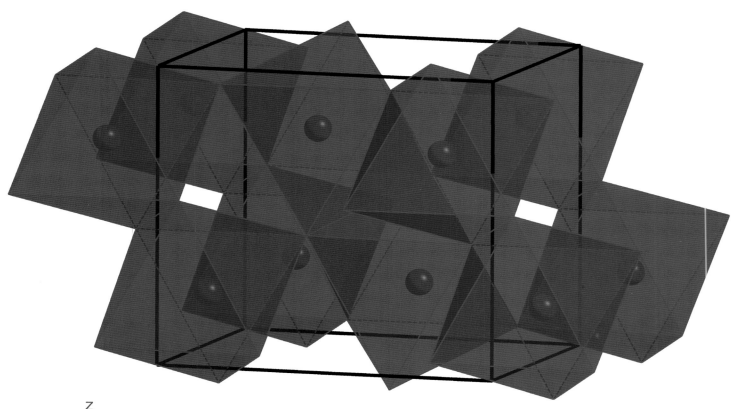

Figure 20. The crystal structure of seifertite, showing octahedrally-coordinated Si, similar to that in stishovite; data from Dera et al. (2002).

Chemistry and color

Silica minerals are intrinsically colorless, so any observable color is created by impurities or inclusions of other minerals, or in the case of opal, from diffraction effects. The causes of color in transparent quartz have been extensively studied; Rossman (1994) provides a detailed review of research up to around 1993. In an early paper, Holden (1925) reviewed early hypotheses concerning the origins of color in amethyst and smoky quartz, and reported his experiments that attempted to show that smoky quartz is colored by atoms of silicon created by radiation-induced breakdown of silica. The modern interpretation, put forward in the mid-1950s, is that the color of smoky quartz is caused by trapped hole centers that are created when quartz that contains some Al^{3+} substituting for Si^{4+} is bombarded by ionizing radiation (Partlow and Cohen 1986).

Figure 21. Tabular smoky quartz crystal ~5 cm long, with smaller crystals, on feldspar from Malawi. *RJL2552*

Figure 22. Smoky quartz crystals to 3 cm long, from the Smoky Bear claim, Lincoln Co., New Mexico. *RJL2297*

The color of amethyst has been attributed to the presence of iron since the work of Woodward in the 1700s (see Dennen and Puckett 1972 for a historical review). It is well known that many amethyst crystals contain inclusions of iron oxides (e.g., hematite, goethite, or lepidocrocite). Holden (1925) found iron in all amethyst samples he analyzed and noted an optical absorption maximum in the 5300-5400 Å region. The color of amethyst was long known to be related to radiation, as it can be destroyed by heating the crystal and restored by irradiation (Dennen and Puckett 1972; Hassan and Cohen 1974; Cohen and Hassan 1974). Cohen (1985) further noted that, "Interstitial Fe^{3+} impurity on the growth-loci of the terminal major rhombohedral faces of quartz protects these regions from becoming smoky-colored if the iron content is in large excess of the Al^{3+} impurity content. ... The oxidation of interstitial Fe^{3+} to Fe^{4+} furnishes an electron for quenching the trapped-hole centers on oxygens adjoining substitutional Al^{3+} sites as they are formed, thus preventing the appearance of smoky color. The resulting amethyst color is due to an absorption band related to the Fe^{4+} produced." He makes the interesting observation that, "Since Fe^{3+} only predominates over Fe^{2+} in natural quartz formed under shallow-growth conditions, usually in cavities or geodes, amethyst color in quartz is limited to these sources."

Figure 23. Pale amethyst enclosing flake-like lepidocrocite, from the Brandberg district, Namibia. *RJL2990*

Figure 24. A richly colored cabinet specimen of amethyst in the "cactus quartz" habit, from Magaliesberg, South Africa. *RJL3857*

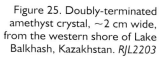

Figure 25. Doubly-terminated amethyst crystal, ~2 cm wide, from the western shore of Lake Balkhash, Kazakhstan. *RJL2203*

Citrine can range in color from yellow to orange and orange-brown. Although naturally occurring citrine is known from several places, most commercial citrine is made by heat treating amethyst. Natural citrine containing Fe^{3+} can sometimes be found as zones of citrine in amethyst; examples include: Hyderabad, India; localities in Minas Gerais, Brazil; and the Anahi mine, Bolivia. In such occurrences, any crystals exposed on the surface may be a combination of citrine and colorless quartz, because the amethyst component has become bleached by sunlight. The cause of color in citrine was originally thought to be substitutional Fe^{3+}; however, Lehmann and Moore (1966) suggested that the color is actually caused by submicroscopic Fe_2O_3 particles dispersed in the quartz. This conclusion was based on similarities of the EPR and optical absorption patterns of natural citrine and artificially heat-treated amethyst. In bicolor amethyst-citrine from India and Bolivia, hydrogen in the citrine zones is mainly molecular H_2O, whereas in the amethyst zones it is predominantly OH⁻ ions (Aines and Rossman 1986).

The Anahi mine, Bolivia, is a particularly notable occurrence of natural bicolor amethyst-citrine, which is called "ametrine" in the gem trade. When the material first appeared on the market in the 1970s, there was some question as to whether it was natural, and Kurt Nassau demonstrated that one could create similar material through a combination of irradiation and heat treatment. However, researchers were able to visit the mine in 1992, and confirmed that the bicolor material is indeed natural, although a complete crystal-chemical explanation for the unusual zoning remains incomplete. From 1989 through 1994, *more than 100 tons of crystals, yielding 40-80 kg/ton of cutting rough*, were produced. Vasconcelos, Wenk, and Rossman (1994) present an in-depth report on this remarkable deposit and the gemological properties of the ametrine that is produced there.

Figure 26. "Ametrine" from the Anahi mine, Bolivia, where rough crystals like this have areas of amethyst and areas of citrine in the as-mined state. Specimen is ~10 cm long. RJL3858

Figure 27. Quartz crystals with a mixture of amethystine and citrine colors, from the Mangyshlak Peninsula, Kazakhstan. *RJL2266*

Rose quartz occurs in two different varieties: Massive rose quartz is found in hydrothermal veins and in granite pegmatites, where it may form part or most of the core zone. Less commonly, it can form isolated euhedral crystals, although such crystals are rarely as sharp as good colorless quartz crystals. The two varieties differ somewhat in their optical absorption spectra, and the massive type is typically cloudy or turbid, sometimes showing chatoyancy or asterism when polished. Because of its importance as an ornamental stone, the origin of color in rose quartz has been studied and debated for many years. Although manganese is sometimes a pink chromophore in silicate systems, Dennen and Puckett (1971) detected no appreciable Mn in several dozen samples they analyzed. They didn't indicate how many of their samples were massive versus euhedral. Goreva, Ma, and Rossman (2001) examined twenty-nine specimens of massive rose quartz from pegmatitic or vein deposits worldwide. In each one, they were able to extract pink nanofibers of dumortierite or a closely related mineral. The identity of the pink chromophore in transparent, euhedral rose quartz crystals remains unsettled. Maschmeyer and Lehmann (1983) identified two new hole centers, one of which is a bridging O^- ion between a substitutional Al and a phosphorus atom. Interestingly, crystals from the Sapucaia pegmatite, Minas Gerais, Brazil, contained 118 P atoms per million Si atoms, and virtually no titanium (another potential pink chromophore). However, Cohen and Makar (1985) examined crystals from the same pegmatite and for a crystal containing 4 Ti atoms per million Si atoms, they proposed charge transfer between substitutional Ti^{4+} and interstitial Ti^{3+} as the coloring mechanism.

Quartz is frequently colored by inclusions of various minerals, such as hematite (red), chlorite (green), etc. Inclusions and associated minerals will be discussed in the entry for quartz in the Minerals section.

Figure 28. Rose quartz crystals associated with pale smoky quartz from Coronel Murta, Minas Gerais, Brazil. *RJL2278*

Formation and Geochemistry

Quartz is a common constituent of many igneous, sedimentary, and metamorphic rocks; it is commonly found in hydrothermal veins, and secondary quartz can form the cementing phase in some sedimentary rocks. Opal can be found in both volcanic and sedimentary environments. Tridymite and cristobalite are generally found in volcanic rocks. The high-density phases, coesite, stishovite, and seifertite are normally restricted to very high pressure metamorphic terrains and situations involving shock metamorphism.

Silica in igneous rocks

Quartz is an essential constituent in many igneous rocks, and indeed the overall mineralogy of igneous rocks depends on whether the rock is over- or undersaturated with respect to silica. Oversaturated rocks contain free silica minerals, whereas undersaturated rocks contain unsaturated minerals such as olivine and feldspathoids. Although it is theoretically possible for a rock to be neither oversaturated nor undersaturated, this condition is quite rare and limited to very localized occurrences (Whitten and Brooks 1972).

In granites and granodiorites, quartz typically forms gray or colorless, anhedral grains. In granite pegmatites, quartz may be a component of "graphic granite" near the pegmatite margin and later form large crystals in the core zone, associated with tourmaline, beryl, topaz, and other desirable species. Occasionally, giant quartz crystals (>500 kg) are found in pegmatites (Jahns 1953).

Figure 29. A colorless to slightly smoky quartz crystal, ~5 cm tall, with a rim of rose quartz along its base, on corroded microcline; a typical pegmatite association, from the Pitorra mine, Minas Gerais, Brazil. *RJL1934*

Hydrothermal quartz veins might or might not be genetically related to pegmatites. They represent mineralizations that crystallized as hot fluids were cooled and became oversaturated with silica. Smith (1958) calculated that if quartz were deposited as a vein filling during a 10°C temperature drop near 500°C, at least 3.75 metric tons of solution must flow through a fissure for each kilogram of quartz deposited. The same process occurring near 100°C would require about 44 metric tons of solution, because the starting concentration of silica in a saturated solution at 100°C is correspondingly lower. If a quartz-bearing sedimentary rock is metamorphosed at 500°C and gives up 2% of its mass as a silica-saturated aqueous solution (representing a real loss of silica of ~1% of the original rock), 1 km^3 of source rock would provide enough SiO_2 for 200,000 metric tons of quartz veins. Such veins, particularly in Brazil, provided most of the raw material for oscillator plates before synthetic quartz took over the market.

Tridymite is typically found in cavities in acid volcanic rocks such as rhyolite, obsidian, trachyte, andesite, and dacite. Cristobalite is formed in similar conditions, sometimes associated with tridymite and sometimes replacing it.

Figure 30. Cristobalite lining a 3-cm cavity in obsidian, from Cougar Butte, Siskiyou Co., California. *RJL4155*

Silica in metamorphic rocks

Quartz is a common constituent of metamorphic rocks, from the lowest to the highest grade of metamorphosed quartz-bearing sediments and igneous rocks. At the higher metamorphic grades, the quartz is typically recrystallized and coarsened. A lot of quartz is produced through the release of silica in reactions that take place during metamorphism, as noted above in the discussion of hydrothermal veins.

Alpine cleft-type deposits are an important source of well-crystallized quartz; they are found throughout the world, but particularly in Switzerland and Russia. These formations are generally found in metamorphic rocks and contain a fairly characteristic mineral assemblage that includes chlorite, actinolite, epidote, muscovite, adularia, titanite, rutile, hematite, fluorite, and other species. The deposits are created when fissures or tension cracks develop during regional metamorphism and the associated hydrothermal solutions enter the fissures, partially dissolving the wall rock and precipitating sharp crystals of quartz and other minerals.

Lechatelierite is found in fulgurites and tektites, both of which may be considered as very specialized cases of localized thermal metamorphism.

Figure 32. A smoky quartz gwindel, 7 cm long, with other terminated crystals on matrix, from Puiva, Subpolar Urals, Russia. *RJL1520*

Figure 31. Very sharp, transparent, smoky quartz gwindel, ~6 cm tall, from Goscheneralp, Canton Uri, Switzerland. *RJL2327*

Figure 33. Doubly terminated smoky quartz crystal from the Mirage Glacier, Mont Blanc, Val d'Aosta, Italy. The termination is slightly frosted with microscopic green inclusions (probably chlorite). *RJL1769*

Figure 34. Two elongated crystals from Mont Blanc, Italy; microscopic red flakes of an unknown inclusion on and in the surface give the crystals a coppery tinge. Specimen is ~ 9 cm tall. *RJL1647*

Figure 35. A 5-cm smoky quartz gwindel from Aiguille des Rochassiers, Bassin de Talefre, Haute-Savoie, France. *RJL2326*

Figure 36. A large cabinet specimen from near Rougemont, North Carolina, in which clear quartz crystals, some included with green chlorite, are associated with pale amber calcite. The sample strongly resembles some Alpine material. *RJL2252*

The high-pressure phases coesite, stishovite, and se-ifertite are typically products of very intense shock metamorphism. Coesite and stishovite are found in shocked Coconino sandstone at Meteor Crater, Arizona, and have since been found at many meteor impact sites throughout the world. At the Kamensk impact structure in the Rostov region, Russia, rocks formed from sandstone at the base of the crater contain as much as 26 wt. % coesite. Unusually large ($\sim$150 μm) crystals of coesite and stishovite were discovered in a structure called the Vredefort Dome, South Africa; the minerals were found in very thin pseudotachylite veins in the Witwatersrand quartzites. The presence of these phases supports the interpretation that Vredefort Dome is an ancient meteor impact structure (Martini 1978).

Coesite is also found in ultrahigh pressure metamorphic terrains. It occurs with pyrope in magnesian quartzite in the Dora Maira massif, Piedmont, Italy, and in eclogites in the Sulu terrain, eastern China, and the Kaghan Valley, Pakistan.

Figure 37. Colorless coesite grains, associated with pink pyrope, in quartzite from the Dora Maira massif, Cuneo Province, Piedmont, Italy. *RJL4165*

Silica in sedimentary rocks

Quartz is a common detrital mineral because it is hard and chemically stable, allowing sedimentation processes to concentrate it into sand and sandstone deposits. Secondary, or authigenic, quartz often crystallizes on the primary sand grains to cement them together. If the sand or sandstone is relatively porous, the secondary quartz often grows epitaxially on the detrital quartz grains, and the boundary between the two generations can only be seen microscopically from rims of iron staining on the original sand grains. The cementation process is much faster in buried sandstones in the water zone, whereas in rocks of similar porosity where oil is present, the deposition of secondary silica can be greatly reduced (Deer et al. 2004).

Chert is a variety of authigenic quartz that normally occurs in massive or stratified form in sedimentary rocks. The world's oldest sedimentary rocks (estimated age 3.5 Ga) are chert; however, there is some debate as to whether these rocks are at least in part the product of hydrothermal alteration and metamorphism (Knauth 1994).

According to Pabian and Zarins (1994), "Agates are sedimentary diagenetic products whose occurrence is related to saline-alkaline conditions, arid climates, and unconformities. The terms chert, thunder eggs, and agates should not be used interchangeably, as each represents a unique geochemical setting."

Agate nodules are found in rhyolitic ash-flow tuffs, e.g., the "thunder eggs" in Jefferson Co., Oregon; in tholeitic basalts, e.g., in Brewster Co., Texas; in andesites, e.g., Moctezuma, Chihuahua, Mexico; in regressive marine carbonates, e.g., in Platte Co., Wyoming; and in continental claystones, e.g., in Sioux Co., Nebraska.

The silica to form thunder eggs in ash-flow tuffs is likely produced as a secondary product of glass devitrification and dissolution. The resulting silica gels percolate downward and collect in vesicles at the base of the tuff layer or in the underlying basalt. Spherulitic crystallization begins when the silica gels contact carbonates and sulfates from high-pH alkaline lakes that had existed on the rhyolite or basalt. Note that thunder eggs are never found in similar but geologically young deposits of tuff over andesite or basalt, whereas in very old rocks, the tuffs may have been completely altered to clays, zeolites, and silica gels, and the underlying rocks are agate-bearing. Air-fall ash is the likely source of silica for agates in continental claystones and in regressive marine limestones, although in marine limestones an organic source of silica can't be ruled out (Pabian and Zarins 1994).

Sedimentary rocks host two forms of quartz that are familiar to every collector, viz., geodes and "Herkimer diamonds." In the Midwestern U.S. geodes occur in limestone of Mississippian age; Keokuk, Iowa, is considered the classic locale for such geodes, but similar formations range through Illinois, Kentucky, Missouri, and Tennessee. Geodes can be found in the limestone or shale as well as weathered out in the soil derived from these rocks. Most geodes have an outer layer of chalcedony and are lined with quartz that is typically colorless. Other minerals that may accompany the quartz include calcite, dolomite, pyrite, galena, millerite, sphalerite, and goethite. Herkimer diamonds are lustrous, doubly terminated quartz crystals found in great numbers near Little Falls, Middleville, Salisbury, and Saratoga Springs in Herkimer Co., New York. Similar crystals occur in sandstone and clay slate in Marmaros, Hungary.

Figure 38. A typical thunder egg from Oregon, ~7 cm in diameter.

Figure 39. A small quartz "Herkimer diamond" in a cavity in limestone, from Herkimer Co., New York. *RJL363*

Figure 40. A large Herkimer diamond cluster from Middleville, New York, with crystals up to 5 cm long. *RJL2314*

Chibaite is formed in marine sediments, and it has been suggested that such clathrasil compounds may be fairly widespread in deep ocean sediments (Momma et al. 2011).

Silica in extraterrestrial rocks

The silica minerals most often found in meteorites are tridymite and cristobalite; quartz is occasionally seen as an accessory mineral in some eucrites.

Tridymite is the most common SiO_2 polymorph in meteorites, and has been noted in: the Rumuruti type R chondrite; the Bouvante eucrite, which also contains quartz; the Steinbach and São João Nepomuceno type IVA irons, which contain numerous rounded pyroxene-tridymite inclusions; and the Gibeon type IVA iron, in which a rare large tridymite crystal was found. Minor or accessory amounts of tridymite are found in basaltic or gabbroic clasts in some mesosiderites (Deer et al. 2004).

Cristobalite is found in some carbonaceous chondrites, and is a minor but widespread phase in some enstatite chondrites. It has also been reported in the Tatahouine achondrite (Benzerara et al. 2002).

Seifertite has been reported in two achondrites: Shergotty, India and Zagami, Nigeria.

Lunar basalts at the Apollo 15 site contain some cristobalite, and basalts at the Apollo 11 site contain minor tridymite. Quartz is rare in lunar rocks, and when found it might represent tridymite that inverted to quartz on cooling. The rarity of quartz on the Moon, compared to Earth, can be attributed to the less-evolved lunar crust and the absence of hydrothermal systems that are responsible for so many crystalline quartz deposits on Earth.

Alteration and pseudomorphs

Because quartz is so widespread in the environment, and SiO_2 is mobile in hydrothermal systems, pseudomorphs have been found in which quartz has replaced many different minerals. The quartz is typically microcrystalline for the case of replacements, and may be more coarsely crystalline for the case of incrustation pseudomorphs or casts. Table 2 presents some examples of pseudomorphs involving quartz.

Table 2. Pseudomorphs by or after silica minerals[a]

Quartz after	Example	Type
aegirine	Mt. Saint-Hilaire, Canada	replacement
analcime	Germany	cast
anhydrite	Brazil	cast
apatite	Malawi	replacement
aragonite	Patagonia, Argentina	replacement
barite	Hüttenberger Erzberg, Austria	replacement
calcite	Romania	cast
danburite	Dal'negorsk, Russia	replacement
elbaite	Minas Gerais, Brazil	replacement
fluorite	Cornwall, England	replacement
glauberite	West Patterson, New Jersey	cast
halite	Tichka, Morocco	cast
ilvaite	Dal'negorsk, Russia	replacement
orthoclase	Mauldenberg, Germany	alteration
pyrophyllite	Starkenbach, Czech Republic	replacement
riebeckite	Griqualand, South Africa	replacement
spodumene	Peru, Maine	replacement
stilbite	Nova Scotia, Canada	replacement

Quartz replaced by		
epidote	Santa Cruz, Mexico	replacement
pectolite	West Patterson, New Jersey	replacement
talc	Göpfersgrün, Bavaria, Germany	replacement

[a]Information largely from issues of *The Pseudo News* (1994-96), published by Philip Betancourt

Pseudomorphs of quartz after calcite are fairly common, and may include both replacements and hollow encrustation pseudomorphs or casts. Replacements of fluorite and barite are also common, especially in hydrothermal veins. Other replacement pseudomorphs have been found of quartz after siderite, rhodochrosite, smithsonite, dolomite, cerussite, aragonite, gypsum, celestine, glauberite, thenardite, anglesite, beryl, datolite, andalusite, laumontite, apophyllite, stilbite, analcime, heulandite, hemimorphite, several amphiboles and pyroxenes, apatite, pyromorphite, scheelite, corundum, garnet, etc. Incrustation pseudomorphs after pyrite, marcasite, bournonite, pyrrhotite, galena, hematite, wolframite, huebnerite, and wulfenite are known (Frondel 1962).

Figure 41. Quartz after bladed anhydrite crystals, ~5 cm tall, on pale, drusy amethyst, from Rio Grande do Sul, Brazil. *RJL2691*

Figure 42. Pseudohexagonal aragonite crystals forming a spherical cluster ~8 cm across, completely replaced by quartz, from Chubut Province, Patagonia, Argentina. *RJL2234*

Figure 43. Rusty, tan, granular quartz replacing a stout apatite crystal, ~4 cm tall, from the Zomba district, Malawi. *RJL2602*

Figure 46. Dark red-brown chalcedony replacing a spherical aggregate of barite crystals, ~5 cm across, from Colorado. *RJL2613*

Figure 44. Prismatic aegirine crystal, ~9 cm long, which has been replaced by gray quartz; a 2-cm smoky quartz crystal is perched in the tip. Specimen is from Mont Saint-Hilaire, Quebec. *RJL2696*

Figure 45. A cabinet-sized specimen of quartz replacing 1-2 cm tabular barite crystals, associated with bright red realgar, from the Julcani district, Angaraes, Huancavelica, Peru. *RJL3088*

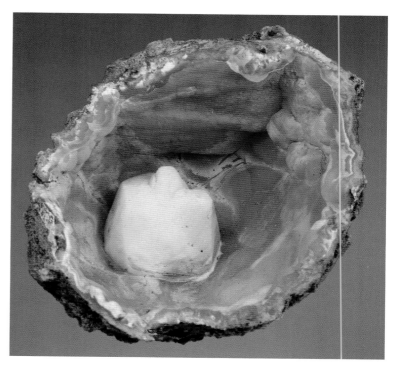

Figure 48. Translucent, colorless chalcedony lining a cavity ~7 cm wide, which contains a sharp white pseudomorph after a calcite crystal that shows two distinct stages of growth. Specimen is from the High Atlas Mountains, Morocco. *RJL2690*

Figure 47. Quartz pseudomorph after octahedral fluorite crystals, from Wheal Mary Ann, Menheniot, Cornwall, England. *RJL2165*

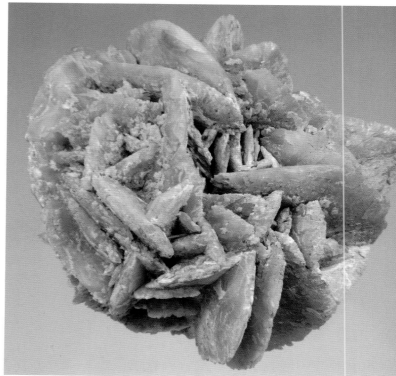

Figure 49. Quartz replacing a cluster of bladed gypsum crystals, from Crawford, Dawes Co., Nebraska. *RJL3152*

Figure 50. Grayish quartz forming a replacement/cast after 2-3 cm apophyllite crystals, from Antelope Flats, Custer Co., Idaho. *RJL3122*

True replacement pseudomorphs of other minerals after quartz are very rare. Two notable examples are the classic occurrence of talc after quartz at Göpfersgrün, Bavaria, Germany, and pectolite after quartz from West Patterson, New Jersey. Incrustation pseudomorphs of various minerals after quartz include hematite, pyrite, cassiterite, goethite, and calcite (Frondel 1962).

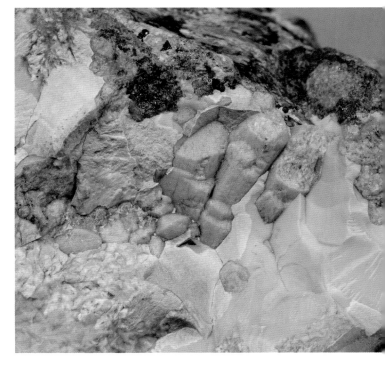

Figure 51. A very old specimen of greenish talc replacing quartz, from Rimpfischweng, near Zermatt, Switzerland. *RJL2336*

Figure 52. Beige talc replacing sharp quartz crystals, from the classic locale at the Johannes mine, Göpfersgrün, Bavaria, Germany. *RJL3300*

The Minerals

Chibaite

Chibaite, a rare clathrasil compound, was described from Arakawa, Minami-Bousou city, Chiba Prefecture, Japan, where it forms crude white crystals associated with another (as yet unnamed) silica clathrate compound in marine sediments of Early Miocene age.

Synthetic silica clathrate compounds are given structural codes rather than names (e.g., MTN, DOH, etc.), somewhat analogous to the practice with regard to zeolites. Chibaite has a structure that is analogous to the synthetic MTN-type silica clathrate compound. The unnamed phase, which is analogous to the DOH framework type, forms thin layers epitaxially on the surfaces of chibaite crystals. Some of the chibaite is pseudomorphously replaced by quartz, and based on the morphology of the pseudomorphs. Momma et al. (2011) suggest that some melanophlogite was likely present when the mineral assemblage was originally formed. These interesting minerals are interpreted to represent traces of low-temperature hydrothermal systems at convergent plate margins, which are the source of natural gas hydrates having similar structures but with ice instead of silica. This suggests that silica clathrate minerals might be much more common than previously assumed, and could be found in many marine sediments.

Figure 53. A thumbnail-sized sample of chibaite from the type locale, Arakawa, Minami-Bousou city, Chiba Prefecture, Japan, consisting of a crust of white, translucent to opaque, intergrown crystals. *RJL4002*

Coesite

Coesite was first known as a synthetic phase, also called "silica C," that was produced by Loring Coes, Jr., at the Norton Company, Worcester, Massachusetts (Ramsdell 1955). It was made by heating a mixture of sodium metasilicate and diammonium phosphate to 500-800°C at 35 kbar pressure for about 15 hours. Sclar, Carrison, and Schwartz (1962) characterized the optical crystallography of synthetic coesite and confirmed its monoclinic nature.

Natural coesite was first reported from Meteor Crater, Arizona, where it is an "abundant constituent" of sheared Coconino sandstone, both in debris under the floor of the crater and in drill samples from ~200 m below the crater floor. It also occurs as a constituent in lechatelierite in the crater. The mineral forms colorless, irregular, 5-50 μm grains (Chao, Shoemaker, and Madsen 1960). By exploiting different rates of dissolution in acids, Fahey (1964) developed an acid treatment process to separate both coesite and stishovite from quartz and glass in ground samples of the sandstone so that purified material was available for study.

Coesite has also been found in high-pressure crustal metamorphic rocks of the eclogite facies: in pyrope-quartzite from the Dora Maira massif, Western Alps (Chopin 1984), and in dolomite-eclogite from the Western gneiss region, Norway (Smith 1984). Ikuta et al. (2007) developed useful methods for performing in situ XRD analysis on thin sections of coesite-bearing eclogite from the Sulu ultra-high pressure terrain, eastern China.

Coesite has also been reported from: Ries Crater, Germany; the Wabar Crater, Al Hadida, Saudi Arabia; the Roberts Victor kimberlite, Cape Province, South Africa, Kentland, Indiana; and Sinking Springs, Ohio.

Cristobalite

Cristobalite was discovered by vom Rath in 1884, during field examination of the locality at Cerro San Cristobal, Mexico, from which the original tridymite specimens had been sent to him several decades earlier. He described euhedral, white, octahedral crystals ~2 mm across and spinel twins to ~4 mm (vom Rath 1887).

Cristobalite is typically formed in volcanic rocks, where it is often found in cavities, in association with tridymite. It is also a component of hollow spherulites (lithophysae) in obsidian, as well occurring in andesite, rhyolite, trachyte, dacite, and basalt. It is frequently a late product of crystallization, sometimes replacing tridymite; associated minerals may include anorthoclase, chlorite, and calcite (Deer et al. 2004). Cristobalite can also be formed by contact metamorphism of sandstones. Cryptocrystalline, disordered low-cristobalite, is an important component of opal.

Cristobalite is widely distributed, with hundreds of documented locales; although it rarely forms large crystals, fine specimens for the micromount enthusiast can be found in many places.

Figure 55. Cristobalite nodules to several cm across, in obsidian from Coso Hot Springs, California. The tiny dark brown crystals are fayalite. *RJL2836*

Figure 54. Detail of the specimen shown in Figure 37: colorless grains of coesite (arrow) in pinkish pyrope, from the Dora Maira massif, Cuneo Province, Piedmont, Italy. *RJL4165*

Figure 56, Off-white spherical aggregates of cristobalite forming a botryoidal layer ~1 cm thick on rhyolite, from the Thomas Range, Juab Co., Utah. *RJL4167*

Notable occurrences include: Nezdenice, Czech Republic; Mayen and Niedermendig, Eifel district, Germany; Sarospatak, Hungary; the Santin mine, Santa Catarina, Guanajuato, Mexico; Ellora, Hyderabad, India; in the Tokatoka district, New Zealand; and the Kosaka mine, Japan. Some U.S. locales include: in andesite near Crater Lake, Oregon; in the Columbia River basalts; in obsidian at Glass Mt., Little Lake, and at Sugarloaf Mt., near Coso Hot Springs, Inyo Co., California; and widespread in Tertiary lavas, e.g., in the San Juan Basin.

Lechatelierite

In 1915, Lacroix proposed the name lechatelierite for natural glasses, particularly fulgurites and meteoritic glasses that closely approach silica in composition. Lechatelierite is not recognized as a mineral species by the IMA, but it is treated here because it is associated with several geological curiosities that are of interest to collectors.

Fulgurites have been known since antiquity; Withering described the connection between fulgurites and lighting in 1790. Fulgurites are formed when lightning strikes soil or sand, and typically form hollow glassy tubes that extend downward by 10 m or more, randomly bending and branching as they go. The outer surface of the tube is normally rough because of adhering sand, and often contains protuberances suggesting the effect of gas pressure when the glass was still plastic.

According to Frondel (1962), "Fulgurites are common. A general condition for their formation is the presence of a dry dielectric such as quartz sand overlying a water-containing stratum or the water table. They are especially abundant or are relatively easily observed in sand dunes, as in the Sahara, and it is estimated that upwards of 2000 fulgurites occur in an area of about 8 sq. mi. in the Kalahari Desert." Myers and Peck (1925) described a fulgurite recovered from a commercial sand pit at South Amboy, New Jersey, and noted that the sample represented what was said to be at least the third fulgurite that had been found there.

Meteoritic glass is formed by the impact of meteorites on quartz sand or sandstone. The most familiar of these materials is Libyan Desert glass, which was discovered and first described by Clayton and Spencer (1934) during a survey expedition of the unexplored area of the Sand Sea and Gilf Kebir in 1932. They recovered about 50 kg of material, including some pieces that had apparently been worked into primitive tools. Analysis showed that the glass is over 97% SiO_2. Clayton and Spencer pointed out the similarity of Libyan Desert glass to tektites, and speculated that the materials were the result of a meteor impact. Lechatelierite has also been reported in numerous tektites, including indochinites, bediasites, and moldavites.

Figure 57. A small fulgurite, ~4 cm long, from Indiana, comprising a hollow tube of fused silica glass (lechatelierite) with sand adhering to the outer surface. *RJL48*

Figure 58. A sample of Libyan Desert glass, ~5 cm tall, from the Gilf Kebir region, Egypt. *RJL3959*

Melanophlogite

Melanophlogite was named by von Lasaulx (1876) in reference to the fact that it tends to turn black on heating. The mineral was described from the sulfur deposits at Racalmuto, Agrigento, Sicily, where it forms small (1-2 mm), glassy cubic crystals encrusting sulfur, calcite, and celestine. Frondel (1962) described it as, "A problematic, pseudomorphous occurrence of opaline silica, chalcedony, and quartz after cubes of an unidentified mineral, perhaps high cristobalite or fluorite." Skinner and Appleman (1963) reviewed earlier research and conducted a number of experiments to determine its structure and properties, before and after heating and grinding. They believed that, "Melanophlogite is a cubic polymorph of silica, less dense than silica glass. The organic matter and sulfur reported in all analyses are due to films of sulfur-bearing organic pigment, trapped on the faces of the crystals as they grew." Later work (Kamb 1965) showed that the mineral is actually a clathrate-type compound, in which organic and other molecules (nitrogen, methane, etc.) are held in large cavities within a polyhedral silica framework. Žák (1972) studied melanophlogite from a 1964-65 find in the Chraletice deposit, eastern Bohemia, Czech Republic, which was originally thought to be fluorite. Žák confirmed the clathrate structure and proposed the formula $46SiO_2 \cdot C_{2.2}H_{17.3}O_{5.4}S_{0.1}$, noting that the Bohemian samples had significantly less sulfur than the Sicilian material. Gies (1983) showed that the high-temperature form is cubic and isostructural with Type I cubic gas hydrates. Na-

kagawa, Kihara, and Harada (2001) determined the crystal structure of the low-temperature tetragonal form, which is a displacive variant of the cubic form. Polarized micro-Raman spectroscopy of guest molecules in material from Mt. Hamilton, California, (Kolesov and Geiger 2003) showed that most of the CH_4 prefers the smaller, nearly spherical cage, whereas CO_2 and N_2 prefer the larger, more oblate cage. Tribaudino et al. (2008) analyzed a new find at Varano Marchesi, Parma, Italy, and found only CH_4 in the clathrate structure. They concluded that melanophlogite had grown at the expense of earlier opal as a result of hydrothermal activity that included a significant influx of methane. They also reported a significant content of H_2S guest molecules in material from the type locale at Racalmuto, Sicily.

The classic U.S. locale for melanophlogite lies in the Franciscan formation of the Mt. Diablo and Coast Ranges in California. The mineral has been found at five places there, with Mt. Hamilton producing the best crystals (Cooper and Dunning 1972; Dunning and Cooper 2002). The mineralization is attributed to near-surface hydrothermal processes at temperatures below about 112°C. Some of the crystals at Mt. Hamilton represent pseudomorphs of chalcedony after melanophlogite, which apparently formed during thirty years of weathering. Skinner and Appleman (1963) reported that melanophlogite converted to cristobalite after heating for a few days at 900-1000°C. Thus, it appears that guest molecules are needed to stabilize the structure, as is the case with chibaite, and when these are lost, the structure collapses to one of the SiO_2 polymorphs.

Figure 59. Polyhedral representation of the structure of melanophlogite, showing the framework of SiO_4 tetrahedra with guest species nitrogen (pale blue balls) and carbon (black balls) representing methane; data from Gies (1983).

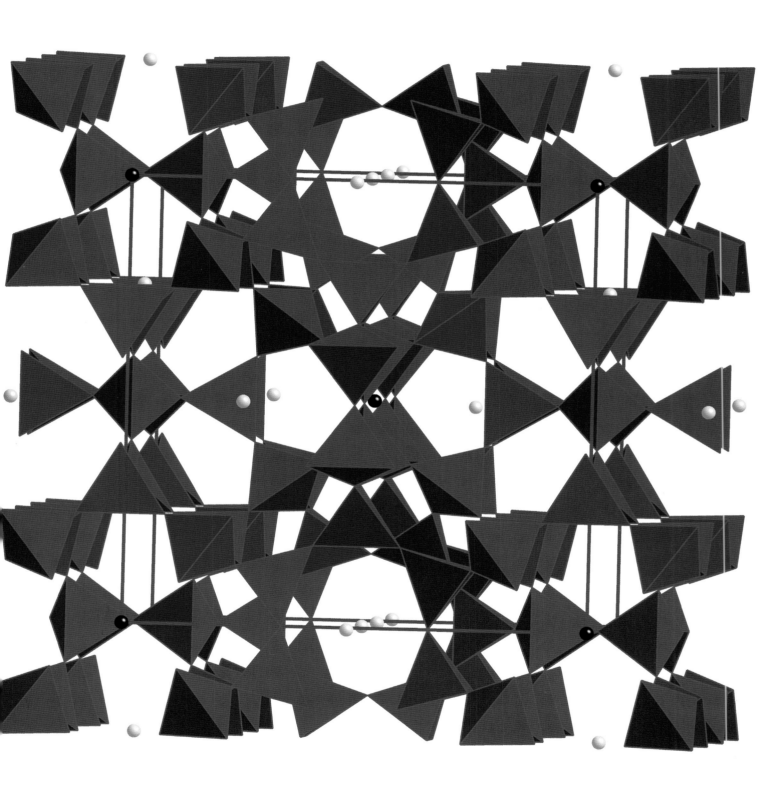

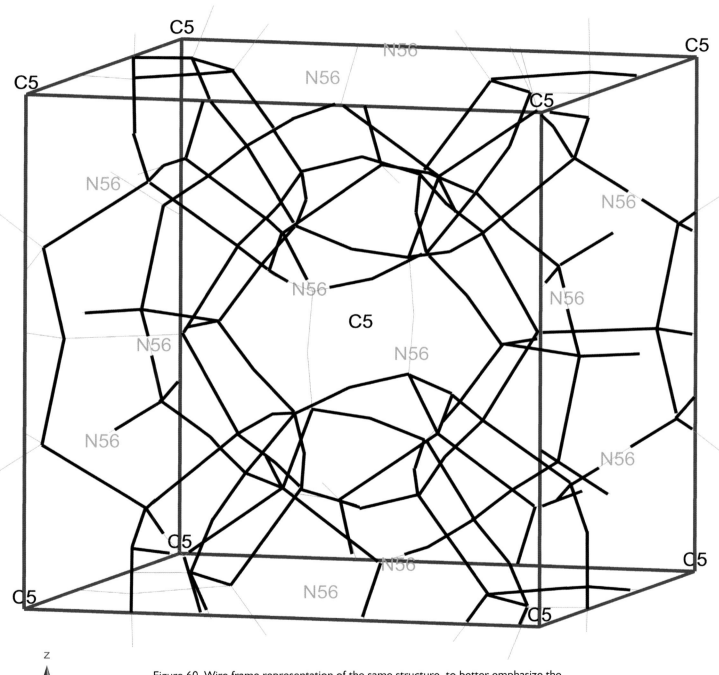

Figure 60. Wire frame representation of the same structure, to better emphasize the cage structure. Methane tends to preferentially occupy the **C5** site in the smaller, more spherical cage in the center and corners of the unit cell, whereas nitrogen tends to prefer the **N56** site, which is a larger, more oblate cage.

Figure 61. A crust of colorless melanophlogite as a thin layer of massive material and small (~0.5 mm) cubic crystals, from the classic locale at a roadcut on Mt. Hamilton, California. Recent reports suggest that the locality is now essentially exhausted. *RJL315*

Mogánite

Fibrous varieties of microcrystalline quartz are called *chalcedony*; typically the fibers are optically length-fast with the z-axis perpendicular to the long axis of the fibers. Michel-Levy and Munier-Chalmes (1890; 1892) coined the terms *quartzine* for length-slow chalcedony when the z-axis lies parallel to the fibers, and *lucetite* when the z-axis lies at about 30° to the fiber axis. Flörke, Flörke, and Giese (1984) determined by XRD that some length-slow chalcedony had a structure that represented a new silica polymorph, which they called mogánite. Godovikov et al. (1991) showed that many samples labeled "lucetite" contain a large proportion of mogánite. Although Gaines et al. (1997) argue that "lutecite" has priority, and treat the mineral under that name, mogánite was later approved by the IMA (in 1999).

The name refers to the type locale at the Mogán formation, Gran Canaria, Canary Islands, Spain, where it occurs in chert nodules within rhyolitic ignimbrites.

Mogánite is evidently fairly common but often overlooked, hiding in plain sight in many chalcedony, flint, and chert deposits. Heaney and Post (1992) studied 150 samples of microcrystalline silica from many localities worldwide, and found some mogánite in virtually every sample. It was noted that mogánite was richest in samples younger than ~100 Ma; over longer times it transforms diagenetically to quartz. Kingma and Hemley (1994) used Raman spectroscopy to characterize a variety of samples from worldwide occurrences, which included chert, flint, chalcedony, and "lucetite." They also found some mogánite in all microcrystalline varieties.

Figure 62. Flattened chert nodule ~4 X 20 mm containing mogánite, from the type locale in the Mogán formation, Gran Canaria, Canary Islands, Spain. *RJL4163*

Opal

Opal is treated separately here, rather than as a variety of cristobalite, following Frondel (1962) who makes the point that, "... x-ray diffraction has shown that opal is not amorphous but is a submicroscopic aggregate of crystallites of cristobalite, containing much nonessential water. Opal is here considered as a variety of cristobalite, standing to that species in much the same relation that chalcedony does to quartz. It is described, however, as if it were a species."

Jones and Segnit (1971) considered a water content of at least 1% to be essential for opal, and proposed a classification system based on the X-ray diffraction pattern:

Opal-C gives a sharp XRD pattern for α-cristobalite and minor tridymite.

Opal-CT gives a pattern with broadened but well-defined peaks for α-cristobalite with varying degrees of stacking disorder, leading to some peaks attributable to tridymite.

Opal-A is X-ray amorphous and gives a very diffuse XRD pattern.

Using a multi-analytical approach, including XRD, IR spectroscopy, and chemical/thermodynamic studies, Langer and Flörke (1974) further subdivided amorphous opal into two types:

Opal-AN has a glass-like structure; this category includes hyalite opal.

Opal-AG has a gel-like structure; this includes many precious opals and "potch" or common opals.

Sanders (1964; 1968; 1975) showed that the play of color in precious opal arises from a regular arrangement of minute spherical silica particles that lie in layers with the right spacing to diffract light. Sanders (1968) examined gem opals in an optical diffractometer and noted several types of diffraction patterns, which he interpreted by analogy to XRD patterns to illustrate the overall structural features, even though the individual particles are too small to resolve in an optical microscope. The particles and their regular arrangement can easily be seen by electron microscopy (Sanders 1975; Fritsch et al. 2006; Gaillou et al. 2008b). Fritsch et al. (2006) showed that transparent orange fire opal that has no play of color is constructed from spherical silica particles ~20 nm in diameter, but the spheres are more or less randomly packed together so that there are no regular planes to diffract light as there are in precious opal. Gaillou et al. (2008b) examined nearly 200 samples of common opal-A and opal-CT and noted that only opal-AN has a texture similar to glass. In opal-AG, the spherical nanograins have a concentric structure. They concluded that, "Common opal does not diffract light because its spheres exhibit a range of sizes, are imperfectly shaped, are too large or too small, or are not well ordered."

Many varieties of opal have been given names based on color or other properties; as with chalcedony, many names are local or trivial variants. Frazier and Frazier (2007b) provide an extensive glossary of opal-related terms. Some of the more important varietal names are the following (Frondel 1962):

Precious opal has a brilliant play of colors in any shade of red, orange, green, or blue, in a translucent to subtransparent body that is usually milky white but may be other colors. *Black opal* has the same play of color, but with a black or dark gray body color.

Fire opal is a type of precious opal with dominantly red to orange play of color and a relatively transparent body color that ranges from yellow or yellowish red to orange or brownish red.

Girasol is a relatively transparent precious opal with a fairly uniform bluish or reddish, wavy or floating play of color.

Common opal is any opal without a play of color or other properties that would give it value as an ornamental stone. This category includes hyalite, milk opal, wood opal, rock-forming opaline silica, etc.

Hyalite opal is glassy and usually colorless, often forming botryoidal crusts, reniform masses, and stalactites. It is sometimes faintly tinted blue, green, or yellowish, and may grade into milky or white opal. Hyalite generally contains less water than most opal and has a higher index of refraction.

Hydrophane is white or pale colored translucent to opaque opal that becomes practically transparent when immersed in water.

Tabasheer is milky white opaline silica deposited inside the joints of bamboo. A dried piece will strongly absorb water and become transparent.

Cacholong is opaque, white to yellowish, with a luster like mother-of-pearl. It is fairly porous but doesn't become transparent when put in water.

Wood opal is common opal in various shades of yellowish to brownish or black, that is the mineralizing material in petrified wood and often preserves details of the wood's grain or vascular structure.

Moss opal contains dendritic inclusions of dark minerals similar to those in moss agate.

The basic conditions necessary for opal to form are, first, a source of silica, and second, some space for the opal to accumulate, either from SiO_2-producing microbes or by evaporation. Such conditions can be found in both volcanic and sedimentary environments. The necessary silica concentration might be as little as 100-200 ppm, which in a volcanic setting might come from hot springs or from hydrothermal alteration of earlier silicates. In siliceous marine ooze, opal is formed from silica derived from radiolarians, diatoms, and siliceous sponges. Overall, the diagenetic sequence is: opal-A (siliceous ooze) → opal-CT (porcellanite) → chalcedony or microcrystalline α-quartz (Deer et al. 2004).

Gaillou et al. (2008a) analyzed gem opals from ten countries to quantify the levels of various impurity elements. They showed that sedimentary opals tend to have Ba > 110 ppm, with Eu and Ce anomalies, whereas volcanic opals have Ba < 110 ppm and no Eu or Ce anomalies. The level of Ca, and to a lesser degree Mg, Al, K, and Nb, can help distinguish gem opals from different volcanic environments. The fact that precious opal has a relatively limited range of all impurity elements suggests that the formation of precious opal requires a more restricted set of conditions compared to common opal.

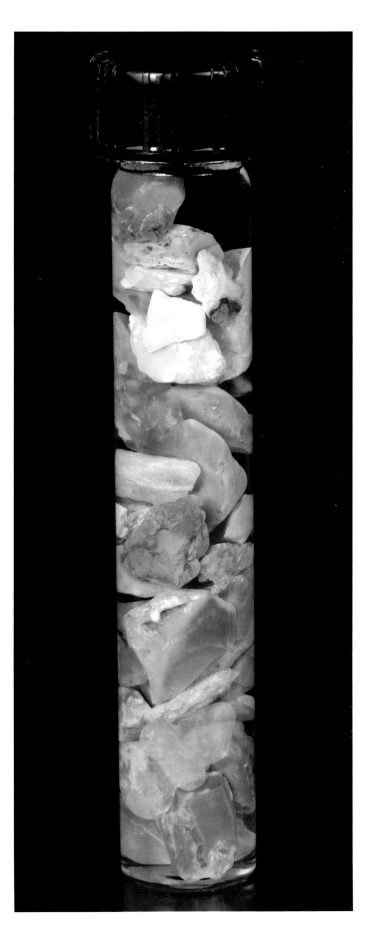

Figure 63. Small pieces of black opal from Lightning Ridge, Australia, stored in a vial of glycerine to better show the play of colors and to prevent dehydration before cutting.

Opal in fossils

Opal is a common preservation medium in fossils, representing permineralization that took place at fairly low temperatures.

Wood opal (also called opalized wood) has a texture or density that can range from soft asbestiform to massive resinous, the latter type being a popular lapidary material because it can take a high polish. Wood opal is also prized by collectors of petrified wood because it often faithfully preserves many of the structural details of the wood. Mitchell and Tufts (1973) studied a large number of samples from worldwide locales and determined that most have the tridymite structure, in contrast to most other varieties of opal, which tend to have the cristobalite structure.

The preservation of fossils by precious opal is a spectacular phenomenon. In an early paper, Etheridge (1897) reported on the finding of a virtually complete plesiosaur skeleton (minus the skull), preserved in opal, from the White Cliffs deposit, western New South Wales, Australia. He described other examples from this occurrence: "The opalized fossils comprise Crinoid remains, the shells of Pelecypoda and Gastropoda, portions of Belemnite guards, and Sauropterygian bones. The preservation of some of these fossils is excellent, although all are not alike in this respect, and the extent to which the opalization has at times been carried is remarkable. In some Pelecypoda, the external growth laminae, and intermediate sculpture striae are fully preserved, whilst the shell substance is completely changed, and by transmitted light the valves of many are almost transparent."

Smith (1999) provides a thorough account of the black opal fossils found at Lightning Ridge, Australia, with photos of several hundred specimens; identifiable fossils include pine cones, crinoids, mollusks, crustaceans, many kinds of fish, plesiosaurs, crocodiles, dinosaurs, birds, and mammals. Pewkliang, Pring, and Brugger (2008) studied the composition and microstructure of opalized plesiosaur bones from Andamooka, South Australia. Based on the textural evidence, they suggest that opalization of the bones occurred in four stages: 1. diagenetic fossilization of the bones, with recrystallization of the biogenic apatite and infill of the Haversian canals by a carbonate mineral; 2. dissolution of the biogenic apatite to form small cavities ($\sim 100 \,\mu$m) in which opal and kaolinite were later deposited; 3. dissolution of the carbonate; and 4. precipitation of chalcedony in canals and cracks. Stages 3 and 4 appear to have been coupled, perhaps accelerated by the shrinkage that accompanies densification of the opal, which might have allowed more fluid flow into the fossil bones.

Figure 64. Gem opal replacing shells, from Coober Pedy, Australia. *RJL2816, 2817, 2815*

Fluorescence

Bright green fluorescence is common in opal, and is attributed to very small concentrations of uranium. Robbins (1994) notes, "Among the brightest of fluorescing minerals is hyalite opal from the vicinity of Burnsville, North Carolina. From the McKinney feldspar mine and the No. 20 mine, it is found as thick crusts of colorless, glass-clear layers and beads that fluoresce bright green. A bluish hyalite is also found there, fluorescing in a less bright green. Similar green-fluorescing hyalite is found at Hyalite Mountain, Montana."

Opal is widely distributed worldwide, with over 2500 reported locales; some notable occurrences of the various types of opal are the following.

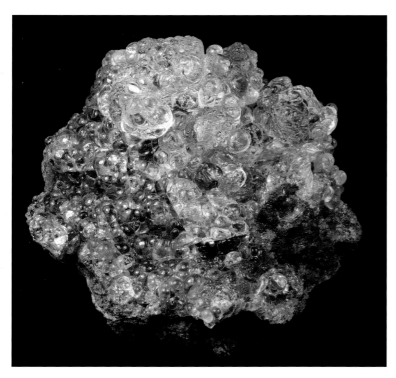

Figure 65. Globular, colorless hyalite opal from Square Top Mountain, near Dalby, Queensland, Australia, covering the face of a matrix ~5 cm wide. *RJL2011*

Figure 66. Specimen in the previous photo, viewed under SWUV light.

Figure 67. Opal on tabular feldspar crystals to ~3 cm long, from the Erongo Mountains, Namibia. *RJL4139*

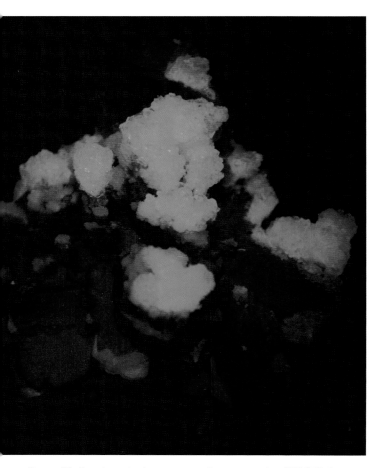

Figure 68. Specimen in the previous photo viewed in LWUV light.

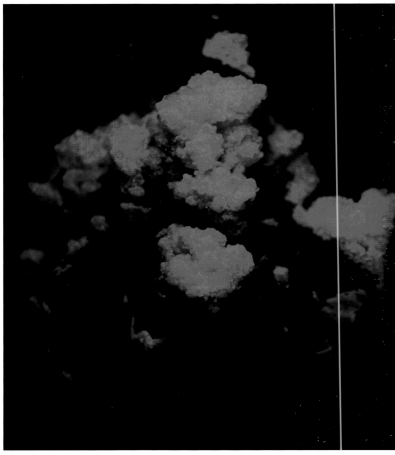

Figure 69. Specimen in the previous photo viewed in SWUV light. Note the more intense yellow-green fluorescence in SWUV as compared to LWUV.

Precious opal mines at Dubnik, near Červenica, in a part of the Hungarian Empire that is now eastern Slovakia, were a very early source of gem opal rough. Although Frondel (1962) states that "Hungarian opal" was known since Roman times, Huber (2007) notes that the Dubnik mines were first specifically mentioned in a mining license granted in 1597. Frazier and Frazier (2007a) cite the confused history of the word *opal*, as it appeared in a 1601 translation of Pliny's *Natural History* (77 AD), and speculate that opal as we know it today might not have been known to the Romans at all. The major deposits in this area lie in eastern Slovakia and in eastern Czech Republic (near Brno), with smaller deposits in Hungary and Romania. These mines encountered competition from Australian discoveries, beginning in the late 1800s, and ceased operation entirely by 1922. Important precious opal deposits in Australia lie in Cretaceous sediments in the Great Artesian Basin, stretching across three states. From west to east, notable localities include: Mintabie, Coober Pedy, and Andamooka in South Australia; Opalton, Yowah, and Quilpie in Queensland; and White Cliffs, Coocoran, and Lightning Ridge in New South Wales (Townsend 2007). In the U.S., some precious opal has been produced in the Virgin Valley, Humboldt Co., Nevada, and near Opal Mountain, San Bernardino Co., California. Honduras has produced precious opal since the mid-1800s and mining continues today at several locales including the Tablon and Las Colinas mines (Dabdoub 2007).

Figure 70. Thin seam of precious opal in dark, glassy fossil wood from the Little Jo Claim, Virgin Valley, Humboldt Co., Nevada. *RJL4160*

Fire opal of very high quality is found near San Juan de Rio, Queretaro, Mexico, as nodular masses in rhyolite. Ethiopia is a recent source of precious and fire opal; material first appeared in 1993-94 and is attributed to an area of ~100 km² in the vicinity of North Shewa, in the state of Amhara, northeast of Addis Ababa (Staebler and Neumeier 2007).

Hyalite opal is of widespread distribution. Important locales include: Valeć, Bohemia, Czech Republic; Puy-de-Dome, France; the Faroe Islands, Denmark; Square Top Mountain, Australia; and Mitchell Co., North Carolina.

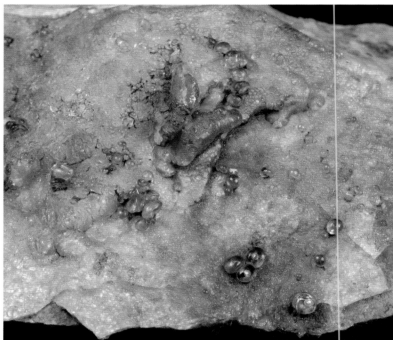

Figure 72. Thin crusts and spherical "drops" of hyalite opal from the classic locale at Valeć, Bohemia, Czech Republic. *RJL4162*

Figure 71. Dark brown opal from North Shewa, Ethiopia, in the typical habit: a 3-cm nodule somewhat like a thunder egg, but instead containing dark amber-brown opal with pinpoint fire. *RJL4154*

Common opal includes a number of forms and habits, ranging from siliceous sinters and geyserites to dense, waxy masses and opalized wood. Siliceous sinter and geyserite are found at Yellowstone National Park, Wyoming; Steam- boat Springs, Nevada; Iceland; and Wairaki, New Zealand. Opalized wood and other common opal is found in Virgin Valley, Nevada, and in Lincoln Co., Idaho.

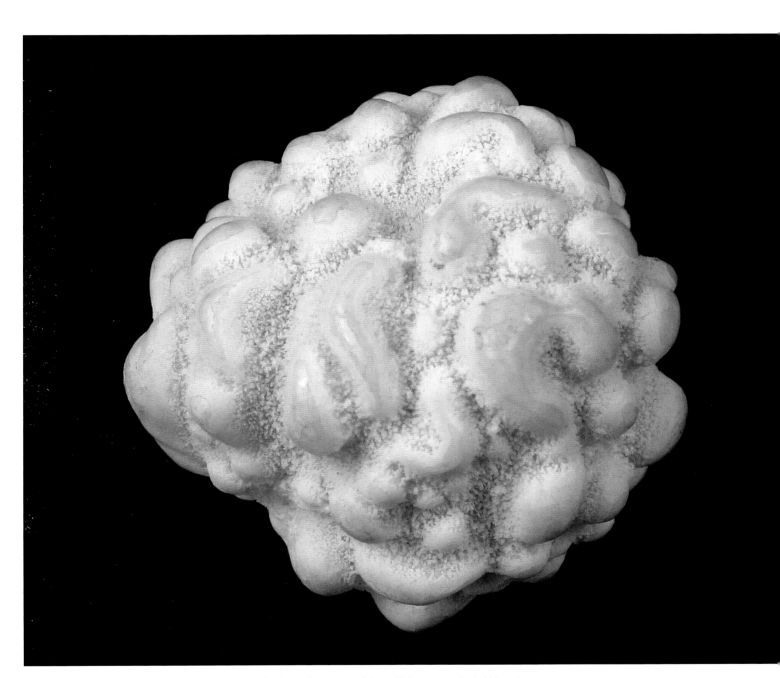

Figure 73. Opal var. *geyserite* in the form of a 1-cm "geyser egg" from Yellowstone Park, Wyoming. *RJL4158*

Figure 74. Common opal from the Virgin Valley, Humboldt Co., Nevada, showing typical conchoidal fracture. This specimen, ~6 cm wide, is fluorescent green in SWUV. *RJL4159*

Figure 75. Common opal filling a small ironstone concretion from the Yowah opal fields, near Eulo, Queensland, Australia. These objects, called "Yowah nuts," are often filled with precious opal. *RJL4161*

Quartz

Quartz is of worldwide distribution in the continental crust. Excellent crystals can be found in many thousands of localities, representing diverse environments, including geodes in sedimentary rocks, sharp and sometimes large crystals in Alpine clefts and hydrothermal veins, and large to gigantic crystals in pegmatites. Jahns (1953) discussed quartz in the context of giant crystals of several species found occasionally in pegmatites. Frondel (1962) further described the sometimes heroic size of some documented examples: "In some areas of Brazil, single-crystals weighing up to 5 tons are abundant and crystals weighing up to 25 tons are not rare. What is probably the largest quartz crystal known was found at Manchão Filipe near Itaporé, Goiaz. It measured about 20 ft. in length and 5 ft. across a prism face, and was estimated to weigh over 120 tons, and yielded about 2 tons of clear quartz. ... A milky white crystal ... estimated to weigh 14 tons was found in a mine near Betpakh-dala in the Balkhash steppe, Siberia."

The great diversity of colors, habits, and associated minerals provides a nearly endless variety of specimen material for the quartz collector. The following sections will attempt to illustrate some of the variety and beauty of quartz with the understanding that the examples are not in any sense comprehensive.

Crystal habits

As noted earlier, twinning is extremely common in quartz; to the casual eye, Japan-law and Dauphiné-law twinning are the most easily recognized. Quartz is also known for abrupt changes in growth that give rise to scepters and inverse scepters. In some cases, the color changes at the same time, providing an even more pronounced contrast between the stem and head of the scepter. Quartz pseudomorphs after many different minerals are also known.

Figure 76. A cabinet specimen from the Pisco-Ayacucho Road, Ica, Peru, containing multiple Japan-law twins. Some of the twins are flattened, whereas others are not tabular but nonetheless show the angles characteristic of Japan-law twinning. *RJL2313*

Figure 78. Amethyst and milky quartz forming a superb scepter, ~5 cm tall, from Hopkinton, Rhode Island. *RJL1419*

Figure 77. Two terminated crystals from Hiddenite, North Carolina, forming a 7-cm tall "V" (possibly a contact twin) with a scepter formation on one of them. *RJL2137*

Figure 79. A cluster of smoky quartz scepters ~9 cm tall, on massive quartz, from Hallelujah Junction, California. *RJL2581*

Figure 80. A miniature-sized specimen of very unusual elongated scepters of gray quartz with darker rims, perched on white calcite, with smaller calcite crystals growing on the scepters, from Santa Eulalia, Mexico. *RJL2365*

Figure 81. An interesting pair of crystals from Tillie Hall Peak, Grant Co., New Mexico, forming a "V" ~11 cm tall; the scepters are each a collection of smaller terminations in parallel. *RJL2080*

Figure 82. A miniature-sized crystal group of amethyst "inverse scepters" from the Tafelkop area, Gobobosebberg, Namibia. *RJL2615*

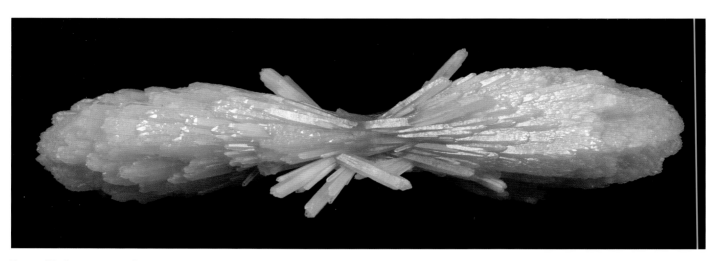

Figure 83. An interesting floater group from the Shangbao mine, Leiyang, Hunan Province, China, in which pale bluish crystals in a sheaf-like arrangement form an elongated "bow tie" ~10 cm across. *RJL2353*

Figure 84. An example of "sawed" or "cut" quartz and datolite from the Bor Pit, Dal'negorsk, Russia. The "saw cuts" are relics of thin calcite wafers that later dissolved away (Moroshkin and Frishman 2001). *RJL3083*

Figure 86. Quartz replacing a 2 X 4 cm ilvaite crystal, associated with elongated quartz and small pyrite crystals, from Dal'negorsk, Russia. *RJL2253*

Figure 85. Colorless quartz forming overgrowths on a papery cast of calcite, from the Verchniy mine, Dal'negorsk, Russia. *RJL2554*

Color varieties

Rose quartz occurs in massive form in many places, including: Rossing, Namibia; the Vorondolo district, Madagascar; and several localities in Brazil. Large deposits are found at a number of pegmatites in the Black Hills. For example, the Scott Rose Quartz mine, on French Creek southeast of Custer, South Dakota, is one of the largest deposits in North America, and at one time had produced more rose quartz than any other mine in the world. According to Roberts and Rapp (1965), "The pegmatite encloses a vein of light to deep-rose quartz 6 to 15 feet thick, 10 to 30 feet high, and several hundred feet in length. One large perfect piece weighing 3,300 pounds and measuring 18 by 30 inches was shipped east and cut into slabs for table tops..." Well-crystallized rose quartz is found mainly in Minas Gerais, Brazil, particularly at Coronel Murta, at the Sapucaia mine, and at Alto da Pitora. Rose quartz crystals up to ~1 cm have also been found at Newry, Maine.

Figure 87. Rich pink group of unusually large rose quartz crystals from Alto da Pitora, Minas Gerais, Brazil, an important locale discovered in 1989 (Cassedanne and Alves 1990). *RJL1354*

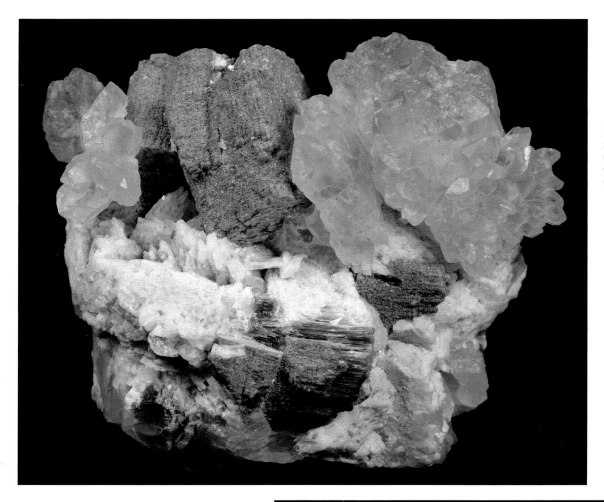

Figure 88. Rose quartz with silvery muscovite on massive quartz/albite, from a pegmatite at Teofilo Otoni, Minas Gerais, Brazil. *RJL2593*

Figure 89. Pale smoky scepters on rose quartz from Coronel Murta, Minas Gerais, Brazil. *RJL2740*

Figure 90. A cluster ~8 cm tall with crystals of colorless, rose, and smoky quartz, from Coronel Murta, Minas Gerais, Brazil. *RJL2651*

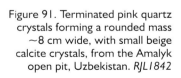

Figure 91. Terminated pink quartz crystals forming a rounded mass ~8 cm wide, with small beige calcite crystals, from the Amalyk open pit, Uzbekistan. *RJL1842*

Amethyst is found worldwide and only a few examples will be mentioned here. Fine material was produced in the Reshev and Alapayev districts near Mursinsk in the Ural Mountains, Russia, and the term Siberian amethyst is often used to describe cut stones of rich, deep color. It has been exported from Brazil and Uruguay since 1727. In Rio Grande do Sul, Brazil, amethyst occurs lining cavities and pipes in weathered melaphyre (amygdaloidal basalt). The resulting geodes are occasionally huge. Frondel (1962) reports that at Serro do Mar a single cavity about 10 X 2 X 1 m was completely lined with amethyst crystals averaging 4 cm across.

Figure 92. Cabinet-sized group of dusky pinkish purple amethyst from Morro Redondo, Goias, Brazil. *RJL1435*

Figure 93. Brilliant, deep purple amethyst group ~10 cm across, from Artigas, Uruguay. *RJL1451*

Figure 94. Rich purple amethyst stalactites, ~5 cm tall, from Artigas, Uruguay. *RJL1456*

Figure 95. A typical amethyst "flower" ~12 cm across, from Irai, Rio Grande do Sul, Brazil. *RJL2614*

Notable Mexican locales include Las Vigas, Vera Cruz; and Amatitlan, Guerrero. The material found at Amatitlan is interesting in that the color zoning is generally darker purple at the base of the crystal and paler or colorless at the tip, which is the reverse of what is usually seen in zoned amethyst.

Figure 96. Amethyst crystal group, ~13 cm tall, from the classic locale at Amatitlan, Guerrero, Mexico. *RJL1401*

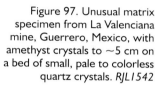

Figure 97. Unusual matrix specimen from La Valenciana mine, Guerrero, Mexico, with amethyst crystals to ~5 cm on a bed of small, pale to colorless quartz crystals. *RJL1542*

Large deposits at Thunder Bay, Ontario, Canada, have been known for over 150 years. In the eastern U.S., numerous locales extend from Maine to Georgia. Sites in Wilkes Co., Georgia, particularly Jackson's Crossroads, have produced extremely large, fine crystals in recent years.

Figure 98. Amethyst crystal ~5 cm across, from Wilkes Co., Georgia.
RJL1450

Figure 99. Amethyst overgrowths on colorless quartz crystals, from Washington Camp, Arizona. The larger crystal is ~7 cm tall. *RJL1834*

Figure 100. An unusual thumbnail-sized specimen in which black, euhedral sphalerite crystals are surrounded by drusy amethyst, from P-vein 2 south, 5 level, Commodore mine, Creede, Mineral Co., Colorado. *RJL3103*

In Africa, some well known amethyst locales include: Brandberg, Namibia; Magaliesberg, South Africa; and a number of pegmatites in Madagascar.

Figure 101. An example of "cactus" amethyst from Magaliesberg, South Africa, in which crystals to 5 cm tall are covered with smaller crystals growing outward along their surfaces. *RJL2594*

Figure 102. Amethyst crystal group ~5 cm wide, from Kuradela, Queensland, Australia. *RJL1355*

Figure 103. A geode ~8 cm in diameter, lined with pale amethyst, associated with brown to black tufts of goethite needles, from Tichka, Morocco. *RJL1460*

Smoky quartz occurs in granites and granite pegmatites at: Oxford and Androscoggin Counties, Maine; Moat Mt., New Hampshire; the Pikes Peak district, Colorado; the Sawtooth batholith, Idaho; on Cairngorm Mt., Banffshire, Scotland; and in the Alto Ligonha district, Mozambique. Fine crystals are found in Alpine clefts and veins at numerous locales in Switzerland.

Figure 104. A 6-cm smoky quartz crystal with feldspar and mica, from a miarolytic cavity in granite of the Sawtooth batholith, Boise Co., Idaho. *RJL1541*

Figure 106. Smoky quartz crystal ~8 cm tall, with a bit of blue microcline attached, from the Blue Smoky claim, Florissant, Teller Co., Colorado. *RJL2553*

Figure 105. A classic association: a 4-cm tall smoky quartz with rich blue-green microcline, from Teller Co., Colorado. *RJL1224*

Figure 107. Doubly-terminated smoky quartz ~3 cm tall with numerous smaller crystals on a small section of geode from Mooralla, Victoria, Australia. *RJL2197*

Citrine can range in color from yellow to yellowish brown, to saffron or honey yellow. There is no clear boundary between yellowish brown citrine and smoky quartz. Natural citrine is fairly rare compared to amethyst and smoky quartz, and it is often found at locales for amethyst, where the crystals contain zones of citrine (Frondel 1962; Gaines et al. 1997). A noteworthy example of this is the "ametrine" found at the Anahi mine, Bolivia (Vasconcelos, Wenk, and Rossman 1994). Some reported localities include: Madagascar; Dauphine, France; Mursinka, Ural Mts., Russia; the Isle of Arran, Scotland; in Brazil at the Morro Redondo mine, Coronel Murta, and at the Morro do Cristal, Campo Belo. Collectors will often see large citrine plates and geodes that obviously began life as the familiar amethyst pipes from Rio Grande do Sul, Brazil, and were heat treated to produce a lovely orange-yellow color. The material is certainly attractive, as long as the buyer understands that the material didn't look like that when it came out of the ground.

Figure 108. Smoky quartz crystal group ~10 cm tall, from Baquachi, Sonora, Mexico. *RJL1514*

Figure 109. A quartz crystal ~5 cm tall from Perekatnoye, Subpolar Urals, Russia, with a color ranging from brownish citrine to smoky. *RJL1643.*

Cryptocrystalline varieties have been given names based on colors, patterns, and modes of occurrence. There are no precise boundaries for these terms, and the materials often grade from one category to another (Frondel 1962):

Chalcedony has a fibrous microstructure, with the fibers generally oriented perpendicular to the layering and to the free surface. It is always porous to some degree, containing isolated pores and tubular or threadlike channels parallel to the fiber direction. Different layers or color bands may have varying amounts of porosity, with white or milky bands being generally less porous. The porosity allows agates to be artificially dyed. Chalcedony is often fluorescent green in UV light because of admixed or adsorbed uranyl compounds. Using transmission electron microscopy, Heaney, Veblen, and Post (1994) demonstrated that there are significant structural differences between microcrystalline fibrous quartz and ideal α-quartz.

Agate is banded chalcedony in which the color and translucency varies from layer to layer.

Onyx is a type of agate in which the bands lie in flat, parallel layers, making it suitable for carving cameos and intaglios.

Iris agate has a periodic structure in which numerous thin bands can diffract light passing through a slice that is cut perpendicular to the banding.

Jasper is massive, dense, dark tile-red to dark brownish red quartz containing up to ~20% of admixed material, mainly iron oxide.

Sard and *carnelian* are varieties of chalcedony colored various shades of light to dark brown (sard) and red to reddish brown (carnelian) by iron oxides; they tend to be more translucent than jasper and more desirable as lapidary materials. Banded sard is called *sardonyx*.

Moss agate is bluish, gray, or white, milky to translucent chalcedony with dark, branching inclusions suggestive of moss, trees, or seaweed. The dark mineralization represents precipitation of oxides of metals such as iron or manganese that diffused into the gelatinous silica before it fully crystallized to form chalcedony.

Chrysoprase is apple-green, translucent chalcedony, apparently colored by particles of hydrous nickel silicate.

Plasma is an opaque green, microgranular or microfibrous variety of quartz. The color has been attributed to inclusions of chlorite, celadonite, and fibrous amphibole.

Prase is leek-green and more translucent than plasma; the color is caused by inclusions of chlorite or fibrous hornblende.

Bloodstone, or *heliotrope*, is a green chalcedony containing red spots of iron oxide or red jasper.

Flint refers to very tough siliceous nodules found in chalk and marly limestone.

Chert is mineralogically very similar to flint, but typically occurs in bedded deposits, sometimes large, that are enclosed in, or interstratified with, limestone, dolomite, or chalk.

Novaculite is a white rock of uniform grain size, wholly composed of microgranular quartz. It may be produced from chert beds by low-grade metamorphism.

Enhydro agates are partially hollow agate nodules that contain water in the central void space. The void is usually not completely filled, so if a window is carefully polished into the wall of the nodule, the water and air bubble can be seen shifting when the agate is tilted back and forth. Collectors must be aware that enhydro agates will inevitably dry up because on a microscopic level the agate is slightly permeable to water molecules and over time the water diffuses out into the atmosphere.

The process by which agates form may be briefly summarized as follows (Pabian and Zarins 1994): Hollow vesicles are formed as gas- or water-saturated lavas solidify. Devitrification of overlying ash-flow tuffs releases free silica, which collects in the vesicles as a gel. The silica crystallizes as spherulites or as fibrous chalcedony, with other mineral phases collecting in troughs formed at the tips of the silica aggregates, creating a banded structure. The banded agate is actually less dense than the original silica gel, so the resulting expansion squeezes the excess silica outward via "escape tubes" (structures that were once thought to represent "filler tubes"). Other minerals such as sulfosalts and transition metal oxides can form sagenitic or crystalline inclusions in the agate; water might subsequently dissolve these inclusions to create hollow molds that can later fill with more silica to create a pseudomorph within the agate.

Agate nodules usually have a pod of euhedral or crystalline quartz in the center. It has been shown that spherulitic chalcedony crystallizes from saturated silica gels, whereas euhedral quartz crystallizes from undersaturated gels, so the boundary between agate and crystalline quartz marks the point at which the silica gel went from saturated to unsaturated states (MacKenzie and Gees 1971).

Agates are found worldwide, and most are named according to their locale or given more fanciful names related to their colors, patterns, etc. For instance, many collectors will be familiar with Mexican agate varieties such as Laguna, Coyamito, Moctezuma, and Crazy Lace. The largest agate deposits in the world are found in southern Brazil, where banded agates are often big enough to be fabricated into slices, bookends, and other finished products.

Figure 110. A sliced agate from Brazil, showing traces of elongated crystals to ~6 cm, (possibly anhydrite) that have been completely replaced by silica. *RJL2235*

Agates from Dulcote Hill, Mendip Hills, Somerset, England, have been known since Roman times, and were plentiful when Dulcote quarry (now closed) was worked for limestone in the 1970s.

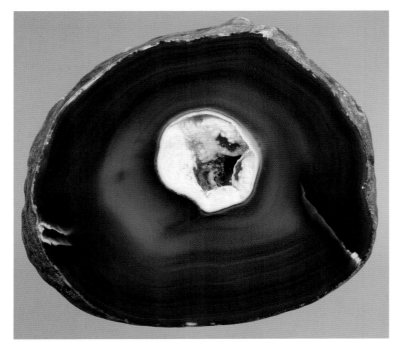

Figure 111. Dulcote agate ~12 cm across, from the Dulcote quarry, Somerset, England. *RJL2022*

Figure 112. Dryhead agate, 12 cm tall, from Montana; the white and colorless bands show intense green fluorescence in SWUV. *RJL1987*

The Patagonia region of southern Argentina has been a prolific source of fine agates since the early 1990s (Strong 1998). There are three basic types of agate, found in separate locales: *Crater agate* occurs in rhyolite at an elevation of ~2000 m in an ancient volcanic crater near Rio Senguer. The chalcedony is typically smoky to black, and usually hollow with bright red hematite lining the interior cavity; bright green UV fluorescence is attributed to uranyl ions. *Puma agate*, found near Gastre, is a pseudomorph after fossil coral. It is typically white with intense red or pastel blue banding.

Figure 113. A Crater agate illustrating the usual combination of translucent dark gray chalcedony highlighted by intense red layers of hematite. *RJL2233*

Figure 114. The sample in the previous photo, viewed in SWUV light. *RJL2233*

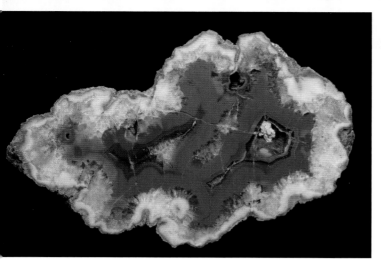

Figure 115. A typical Puma agate, showing contrasting bands of red and white. *RJL2232*

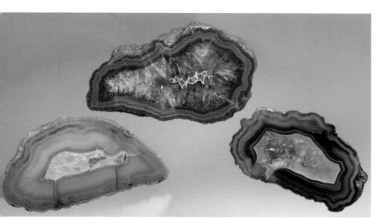

Figure 116. A selection of Condor agates showing some of the range of colors and structures. Two of the pieces have crystalline quartz in the centers, whereas the sample on the left is filled with calcite. *RJL 2273, 2276, 2274*

Figure 117. A large and richly colored Condor agate with a core of white calcite. *RJL2231*

Some pieces are fluorescent as well. *Condor agate*, found near Esquel, displays a rich variety of colors and patterns. Some Condor agates have colorless, coarsely crystalline quartz in the center; others contain massive calcite.

Agatized coral has been known from the Ballast Point area of Tampa Bay, Florida, since the 1800s. In the typical specimen, hollow coral is partially filled with transparent chalcedony in various shades from black to reddish amber, or with cream to white common opal. The coral is generally associated with Tertiary marine sedimentary formations from the eastern Florida Panhandle and nearby southern Georgia through central and west Florida, as far south as Sarasota County. Calcified corals have been found in several southern Florida localities. Many deposits seem to occur in upper Oligocene to lower Miocene shallow marine limestones and marls. With rare exceptions, most collectible strata are below the present surface, and are exposed along river channels or as a result of dredging and other excavations (Gary Maddox, *personal communication*).

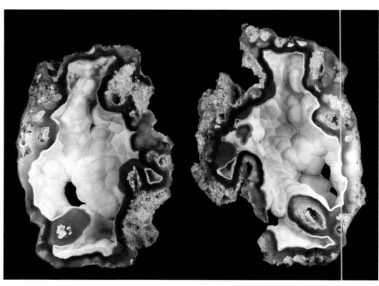

Figure 118. Polished halves of an agatized coral head ~12 X 18 cm, from Tampa Bay, Florida.

Inclusions

Quartz, being normally transparent and intrinsically colorless, often shows visible inclusions of various minerals. In some cases, such as iron oxides and chlorite, the inclusions are microscopic or earthy and create either a uniform color or sharp phantoms. When the inclusions are needle-like and colorful, e.g., rutile, epidote, and tourmaline, the material may be used for faceted gems or cabochons. In other cases, the inclusions create interesting collector specimens and provide insights into the geochemical environment in which the quartz crystallized. In this regard, fluid inclusions are especially important and useful, as they might contain water, CO_2, traces of gases such as nitrogen or methane, dissolved salts such as NaCl or $CaCl_2$, and minute crystals of halite or other minerals. Most fluid inclusions contain small bubbles, which formed on cooling; in other words, when a crystal first forms, the internal cavity is completely filled with liquid, and as the rock proceeds to cool, the liquid contracts, leaving behind a partial vacuum that looks like an air bubble. Often, the sample can be carefully re-heated while observing the bubble in a microscope. The bubble will disappear when the sample reaches the original crystallization temperature because the fluid will have expanded to fill the entire cavity. This "homogenization temperature" can also be used to study inclusions in which some or all of the liquid is actually liquid CO_2 at high pressure. Further, when the liquid contains tiny salt crystals, the temperature at which these crystals dissolve provides a measure of the salinity of the original fluid (Zacharias et al. 2005).

Figure 119. A quartz crystal, ~5 cm tall, on white albite, from the Arthur Costa mine, Jaguaraçu, Minas Gerais, Brazil. The quartz is thickly included with black tourmaline needles. *RJL2178*

Figure 120. A fine example of rutilated quartz, from the Hardangervidda region, Norway. *RJL2242*

Figure 121. Green, chlorite-included quartz crystals, associated with white calcite, from Santa Eulalia, Mexico. *RJL3855*

Figure 123. Quartz containing blood-red hematite inclusions, covered by a thin transparent overgrowth, from Gertis, Orange River area, Namibia. *RJL2683*

Figure 122. Drusy amethyst from Thunder Bay, Ontario, colored red by tiny blebs of hematite. *RJL90*

Figure 124. A cabinet-sized sample of red quartz, colored by hematite, from the Julius Sauer mine, Minas Gerais, Brazil. *RJL3132*

Figure 127. Silvery gray needles of stibnite in colorless quartz, from Rye Patch, Pershing Co., Nevada. *RJL2903*

Figure 125. Bright red quartz crystal group, ~4 cm tall, colored by iron oxides, from the Nikolaevskiy mine, Dal'negorsk, Russia. *RJL2908*

Figure 128. A thumbnail-sized quartz crystal from Ketsaketsa, Madagascar, containing black hollandite in small radiating groups. *RJL2683*

Figure 126. Detail of the sample shown earlier in Fig. 23: colorless to slightly amethystine quartz from Brandberg, Namibia, with red flake-like inclusions of an iron oxide, typically identified as lepidocrocite. *RJL2990*

Figure 129. Amethyst crystal from Brandberg, Namibia, containing a fluid-filled cavity or "negative crystal" containing a small bubble. Note also the sharp color zoning. *RJL2186*

Seifertite

Seifertite was described from the Shergotty, India, basaltic achondrite, which fell in 1865; it has also been reported in the Zagami, Nigeria, achondrite; both meteorites are believed to represent Martian rocks. The phase was first reported by Sharp et al. (1999) and its structure was confirmed by Dera et al. (2002).

The Shergotty meteorite consists of ~70% pyroxene and 24% glass of labradorite composition. Silica grains, up to ~900 μm across, are usually enclosed in the glass phase. The silica grains contain seifertite lamellae, intergrown with minor stishovite and another SiO_2 polymorph (presently unnamed) that has the monoclinic α-ZrO_2 (baddeleyite) structure. The formation of seifertite is attributed to shock-induced solid-state transformation of either tridymite or cristobalite on Mars (El Goresy et al. 2008).

Seifertite represents the densest (ρ=4.295) and hardest polymorph of silica found in nature. Its structure is similar to that of α-PbO_2. It is stable at pressures >780 kbar, so if free silica were present in the earth's mantle, this phase could theoretically form at depths >1,700 km.

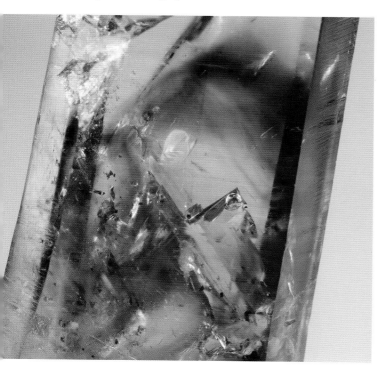

Figure 130. Detail of the sample in the previous photo, taken from the rear, showing the bubble at the top of a somewhat irregular cavity that is nearly 1 cm long.

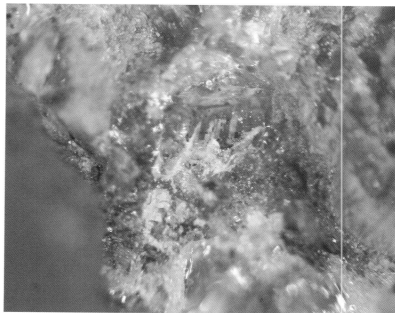

Figure 131. Small laths of crystalline material within the glassy phase in a fragment of the Zagami meteorite. It is in this sort of material that seifertite and the unnamed silica polymorph may be found.

Stishovite

Stishovite, like coesite, was created in the laboratory and later identified in the shocked sandstone at Meteor Crater, Arizona. The original synthesis was carried out in 1961 by Stishov and Popova, who reported the conditions as 1200-1400°C and pressure >160 kbar; it was later suggested that the actual pressure could have been 30% lower because of calibration errors. Stishovite is much more dense than coesite or quartz (ρ=4.285 versus 2.93 and 2.65, respectively), owing to the fact that the Si is in octahedral rather than tetrahedral coordination. It was the first mineral found to have octahedrally coordinated silicon, and because it is isostructural with rutile, some authors place it in the rutile group instead of with the silicates (Gaines et al. 1997). Compared to other rutile-type oxides, stishovite has the highest polyhedral bulk modulus. Any free silica in the earth's mantle is expected to be in the form of stishovite (or seifertite, depending on depth) (Ross et al. 1990).

At the type locale, stishovite forms colorless, submicron-sized grains associated with coesite and lechatelierite (Chao et al. 1962). It has also been identified at: Ries Crater, Germany; the Popigai impact structure, Siberia; the Lonar Crater, India; and Vredefort Dome, South Africa.

Figure 132. Shocked Coconino sandstone, ~2 X 4 cm, from Meteor Crater, Arizona, the type locale for stishovite and coesite. *RJL4168*

Tridymite

Tridymite was originally described from Cerro San Cristobal, near Pachuca, Mexico, where it occurs in andesite (trachyte porphyry). The name alludes to its tendency to form twinned crystals in the shape of trillings (vom Rath 1868). Once it was accurately described, tridymite was quickly identified at other locales; synthetic material prepared earlier was shown to be tridymite as well (Frondel 1962). Tridymite forms small colorless to white crystals and twins, many of which have subsequently transformed to quartz. These pseudomorphs tend to be opaque, milky white, with a granular structure. The quartz often tends to have a definite orientation relative to the original tridymite crystal (Frondel 1962).

Tridymite typically forms in acid volcanic rocks such as rhyolite, obsidian, trachyte, andesite, and dacite, and is sometimes found in basalt. In these rocks the tridymite is usually found in cavities, where it might be associated with sanidine, augite, or fayalite (Deer et al. 2004). In the rhyolitic tuffs of the western U.S., tridymite is abundant and actually makes up the binding phase that formed after the tuffs were deposited. In these rhyolites and quartz latites, tridymite is the primary silica mineral, forming as much as 25% of the rocks. Larsen et al. (1936) estimated that, "the quantity of tridymite in the San Juan lavas is 350 cubic miles, or enough to cover the State of Massachusetts with a uniform layer 250 feet thick. The quantity of quartz is nearly as great as that of tridymite."

Figure 133. Clusters of tridymite crystals ~2-3 mm wide, from Vechec, Northern Slanske Mountains, Presov region, Slovakia. *RJL3092*

Tridymite can also form as a result of high-temperature contact metamorphism, in which silica is introduced from the intruding igneous magma; it has also been found in paralava associated with burning coal seams. It is the most common form of silica in meteorites, being documented in chondrites, eucrites, mesosiderites, and irons. Tridymite is also found in some lunar basalts from the Apollo 11 site.

Tridymite is of worldwide distribution, with over 300 documented locales. In addition to the type locale near Pachuca, Mexico, some notable occurrences include: in trachytes of the Siebengebirge, Rhineland, Germany; at San Piero Montagnone and elsewhere in the Euganean Hills, Padua, Italy; Puy-de-Dome, France; the Vechec quarry, Slovakia; Summit Rock, Klamath Co., Oregon; and Portola, Plumas Co., California.

Figure 134. Crude, 2-3 mm tabular tridymite crystals in a cavity in felsic rock, from San Piero Montagnone, in the Euganean Hills, Padua, Italy. *RJL4164*

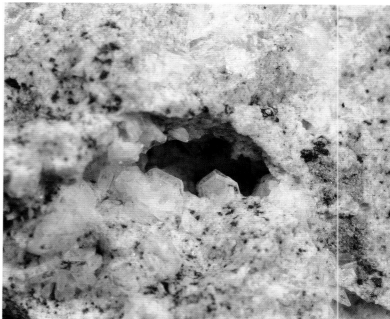

Figure 136. Tridymite crystals to ~2 mm in vugs in weathered andesite, from Smith Peak Road, north of Portola, Plumas Co., California. *RJL4170*

Figure 135. Minute glassy tridymite crystals forming drusy coatings in vugs, from Kajia-Kanagawa-Ken, Honshu Island, Japan. *RJL4169*

References

In addition to the references cited, readers interested in a comprehensive scientific review of the silica minerals might consider the book, *Silica: Physical Behavior, Geochemistry, and Materials Applications*, Reviews in Mineralogy and Geochemistry Vol. 29, P.J. Heaney, C.T. Prewitt and G.V. Gibbs, editors, available from the Mineralogical Society of America (1994). This volume of review papers, citing thousands of original references and reports, clearly shows the complexity of the silica minerals and their importance to the science of petrology and geochemistry. In a more recent scientific review, Deer et al. (2004) devote 152 pages to silica minerals.

Aines, R. D. and G. R. Rossman 1986. Relationships between radiation damage and trace water in zircon, quartz, and topaz. *American Mineralogist* 71: 1186-93.

Araki, T. and T. Zoltai 1969. Refinement of a coesite structure. *Zeitschrift für Kristallographie* 129: 381-87.

Benzarara, K., F. Guyot, J. A. Barrat, P. Gillet, and M. Lesourd 2002. Cristobalite inclusions in the Tatahouine achondrite: Implications for shock conditions. *American Mineralogist* 87: 1250-56.

Bloss, F. D. and G. V. Gibbs 1963. Cleavage in quartz. *American Mineralogist* 48: 821-38.

Cassedanne, J. P. and J. Alves 1990. Crystallized rose quartz from Alto da Pitora, Minas Gerais, Brazil. *Mineralogical Record* 21 (5): 409-12.

Chao, E. C. T., E. M. Shoemaker, and B. M. Madsen 1960. First natural occurrence of coesite. *Science* 132: 220-2.

Chao, E. C. T., J. J. Fahey, J. Littler, and D. J. Milton 1962. Stishovite, SiO₂, a very high pressure new mineral from Meteor Crater, Arizona, *Journal of Geophysical Research* 67 (1): 419–21.

Chopin, C. 1984. Coesite and pure pyrope in high-grade blueschists of the Western Alps: a first record and some consequences. *Contributions to Mineralogy and Petrology* 86: 107-18.

Clayton, P. A. and L. J. Spencer 1934. Silica-glass from the Libyan Desert. *Mineralogical Magazine* 23: 501: 8.

Cohen, A. J. 1985. Amethyst color in quartz, the result of radiation protection involving iron. *American Mineralogist* 70: 1180-85.

Cohen, A. J. and F. Hassan 1974. Ferrous and ferric ions in synthetic α-quartz and natural amethyst. *American Mineralogist* 59: 719-28.

Cohen, A. J. and L. N. Makar 1985. Dynamic biaxial absorption spectra of Ti^{3+} and Fe^{3+} in a natural rose quartz crystal. *Mineralogical Magazine* 49: 709-15.

Cooper, J. F. and G. E. Dunning 1972. Melanophlogite from Mount Hamilton, Santa Clara County, California. *American Mineralogist* 57: 1494-1504.

Dabdoub, T. 2007. Honduran precious opal. *extraLapis English* 10: 75.

Deer, W. A., R. A. Howie, and J. Zussman 1992. *An Introduction to the Rock-Forming Minerals*, Second Edition, Harlow: Pearson Prentice Hall, 696 pp.

Deer, W. A., R. A. Howie, W. S. Wise, and J. Zussman 2004. *Rock-Forming Minerals, Volume 4B, Framework Silicates: Silica Minerals, Feldspathoids, and the Zeolites*, Second Edition, London: The Geological Society, 982 pp.

Dennen, W. H. and A. M. Puckett 1971. On the chemistry and color of rose quartz. *Mineralogical Record* 2 (5): 226-7.

Dennen, W. H. and A. M. Puckett 1972. On the chemistry and color of amethyst. *Canadian Mineralogist* 11: 448-56.

Dera, P., C. T. Prewitt, N. Z. Boctor, and R. J. Hemley 2002. Characterization of a high-pressure phase of silica from the Martian meteorite Shergotty. *American Mineralogist* 87: 1018-23.

Dollase, W. A. 1965. Reinvestigation of the structure of low cristobalite. *Zeitschrift für Kristallographie* 121: 369-77.

Dolley, T. P. 2011. Silica. *2009 Minerals Yearbook*, U. S. Geological Survey.

Dunning, G. E. and J. F. Cooper 2002. Pseudomorphic melanophlogites from California. *Mineralogical Record* 33 (3): 237-42.

El Goresy, A., P. Dera, T. G. Sharp, C. T. Prewitt, M. Chen, L. Dubrovinsky, B. Wopenka, N. Z. Boctor, and R. J. Hemley 2008. Seifertite, a dense orthorhombic polymorph of silica from the Martian meteorites Shergotty and Zagami. *European Journal of Mineralogy* 20: 523-28 [see abstract (2009) *American Mineralogist* 94: 403].

Etheridge, R. 1897. An Australian Sauropterygian (Cimoliosaurus), converted into precious opal. *Records of the Australian Museum* 3: 19-29.

Fahey, J. J. 1964 Recovery of coesite and stishovite from Coconino sandstone of Meteor Crater, Arizona. *American Mineralogist* 49: 1643-47.

Flörke, O. W., U. Flörke, and U. Giese 1984. Moganite: a new microcrystalline silica-mineral. *Neues Jahrbuch für Mineralogie Abhandlungen* 149: 325-36 [see abstract (1985) *American Mineralogist* 70: 874].

Frazier, S. and A. Frazier 2007a. The opal enigma: science, history, and lore. *extraLapis English* 10: 6-11.

Frazier, S. and A. Frazier 2007b. An opal glossary of terms. *extraLapis English* 10: 52-63.

Fritsch, E., E. Gaillou, B. Rondeau, A. Barreau, D. Albertini, and M. Ostroumov 2006. The nanostructure of fire opal. *Journal of Non-Crystalline Solids* 352: 3957-60.

Frondel, C. 1945. Secondary Dauphiné twinning in quartz. *American Mineralogist* 30: 447-68.

Frondel, C. 1962. *The System of Mineralogy*, Seventh edition, Volume III. New York: Wiley, 334 pp.

Gaillou, E., A. Delaunay, B. Rondeau, M. Bouhnik-le-Coz, E. Fritsch, G. Cornen, and C. Monnier 2008a. The geochemistry of gem opals as evidence of their origin. *Ore Geology Reviews* 34 (1-2): 113-26.

Gaillou, E., E. Fritsch, B. Aguilar-Reyes, B. Rondeau, J. Post, A. Barreau, and M. Ostroumov 2008b. Common gem opal: An investigation of micro- to nanostructure. *American Mineralogist* 93: 1865-73.

Gaines, R.V., H. C. W. Skinner, E. E. Foord, B. Mason, and A. Rosenzweig 1997. *Dana's New Mineralogy*, Eighth Edition, New York: Wiley.

Gault, H. R. 1949. The frequency of twin types in quartz crystals. *American Mineralogist* 34: 142-62.

Gibbs, G. V., C. T. Prewitt, and K. J. Baldwin 1977. A study of the structural chemistry of coesite. *Zeitschrift für Kristallographie* 145: 108-23.

Gies, H. 1983. Studies on clathrasils. III. Crystal structure of melanophlogite, a natural clathrate compound of silica. *Zeitschrift für Kristallographie* 164: 247-57.

Godovikov, A. A., S. N. Nenasheva, V. S. Pavlyuchenko, and O. I. Ripinen 1991. New Finds of lucetite. *Doklady Akademie Nauk SSSR* 320: 428-33 [see abstract (1993) *American Mineralogist* 78: 236].

Goldschmidt, V. 1922. *Atlas der Krystallformen* Vol. VII [see Facsimile Reprint in Nine Volumes (1986) by the Rochester Mineralogical Symposium].

Goreva, J. S., C. Ma, and G. R. Rossman 2001. Fibrous nanoinclusions in massive rose quartz: The origin of rose coloration. *American Mineralogist* 86: 466-72.

Hassan, F. and A. J. Cohen 1974. Biaxial color centers in amethyst quartz. *American Mineralogist* 59: 709-18.

Heaney, P. J. 1994. Structure and chemistry of the low-pressure silica polymorphs. *Reviews in Mineralogy* 29: 1-40.

Heaney, P. J. and J. E. Post 1992. The widespread distribution of a novel silica polymorph in microcrystalline quartz varieties. *Science* 255: 441-3.

Heaney, P. J. and J. E. Post 2001. Evidence for an *I2/a* to *Imab* phase transition in the silica polymorph mogánite at ~570 K. *American Mineralogist* 86: 1358-66.

Heaney, P. J., D. R. Veblen, and J. E. Post 1994. Structural disparities between chalcedony and macrocrystalline quartz. *American Mineralogist* 79: 452-60.

Hemley, R. J., C. T. Prewitt, and K. J. Kingma 1994. High pressure behavior of silica. *Reviews in Mineralogy* 29: 41-81.

Holden, E. F. 1925. The cause of color in smoky quartz and amethyst. *American Mineralogist* 10: 203-52.

Huber, P. 2007. Classic Slovakia. *extraLapis English* 10: 12-3.

Hurlbut, C. S., Jr. and G. S. Switzer 1979. *Gemology.* New York: John Wiley & Sons.

Ikuta, D., N. Kawame, S. Banno, T. Hirajima, K. Ito, J. F. Rakovan, R. T. Downs, and O. Tamada 2007. First in situ X-ray identification of coesite and retrograde quartz on a glass thin section of an ultrahigh-pressure metamorphic rock and their crystal structure details. *American Mineralogist* 92: 57-63.

Jahns, R. H. 1953. The genesis of pegmatites. I. Occurrence and origin of giant crystals. *American Mineralogist* 38: 563-98.

Jones, J. B. and E. R. Segnit 1971. The nature of opal. I. Nomenclature and constituent phases. *Journal of the Geological Society of Australia* 18: 57-68.

Kamb, B. 1965. A clathrate crystalline form of silica. *Science* 148: 232-4.

Kingma, K. J. and R. J. Hemley 1994. Raman spectroscopic study of microcrystalline silica. *American Mineralogist* 79: 269-73.

Knauth, L. P. 1994. Petrogenesis of chert. *Reviews in Mineralogy* 29: 233-58.

Koivula, J. I. and E. Fritsch 1989. The growth of Brazil-twinned synthetic quartz and the potential for synthetic amethyst twinned on the Brazil law. *Gems & Gemology* 25 (3): 159-64.

Kolesov, B. A. and C. A. Geiger 2003. Molecules in the SiO$_2$-clathrate melanophlogite: A single-crystal Raman study. *American Mineralogist* 88: 1364-68.

Langer, K. and O. W. Flörke 1974. Near infrared absorption spectra (4000 - 9000 cm^{-1}) of opals and the role of water in these SiO$_2$·nH$_2$O minerals. *Fortschrifte der Mineralogie* 52: 17-51.

Larsen, E. S., J. Irving, F. A. Gonyer, and E. S. Larsen III 1936. Petrologic results of a study of the minerals from the Tertiary volcanic rocks of the San Juan region, Colorado. *American Mineralogist* 21: 679-701.

Lehmann, G. and W. J. Moore 1966. Optical and paramagnetic properties of iron centers in quartz. *Journal of Chemical Physics* 44: 1741-45.

MacKenzie, F. T. and R. Gees 1971. Quartz: Synthesis at earth-surface conditions. *Science* 173: 533-35.

Martini, J. E. J. 1978. Coesite and stishovite in the Vredefort Dome, South Africa. *Nature* 272: 715-17.

Maschmeyer, D. and G. Lehmann 1983. A trapped-hole center causing rose coloration of natural quartz. *Zeitschrift für Kristallographie* 163 (3-4): 181-96.

McLaren, A. C. and D. R. Pitkethly 1982. The twinning microstructure and growth of amethyst quartz. *Physics and Chemistry of Minerals* 8: 128-35.

Michele-Lévy, A. and C. P. E. Munier-Chalmas 1890. Sur de nouvellesformes de silice cristallisee. *Comptes Rendus de l'Academie des Sciences de Paris* 110: 649-52.

Michele-Lévy, A., and C. P. E. Munier-Chalmas 1892. Memoire sur diverses formes affectees par le reseau elementaire du quartz. *Bulletin de la Societe français de Mineralogie* 15: 159-90.

Mitchell, R. S., and S. Tufts 1973. Wood opal – A tridymite-like mineral. *American Mineralogist* 58: 717-20.

Momma, K., T. Ikeda, K. Nishikubo, N. Takahashi, C. Honma, M. Takada, Y. Furukawa, T. Nagase, and Y. Kudoh 2011. New silica clathrate minerals that are isostructural with natural gas hydrates. *Nature Communications* 2: 196.

Moroshkin, V. V. and N. I. Frishman 2001. Dal'negorsk: Notes on mineralogy, *Mineralogical Almanac,* Vol. 4. Moscow: Ocean Pictures, Ltd.

Myers, W. M. and A. B. Peck 1925. A fulgurite from South Amboy, New Jersey. *American Mineralogist* 10: 152-5.

Nakagawa, T., K. Kihara, and K. Harada 2001. The crystal structure of low melanophlogite. *American Mineralogist* 86: 1506-12.

Nassau, K. 1980. *Gems made by man.* Santa Monica: Gemological Institute of America.

Nukui, A., H. Nakazawa, and M. Akao 1978. Thermal changes in monoclinic tridymite. *American Mineralogist* 63: 1252-59.

Pabian, R. K. and A. Zarins 1994. Banded agates: Origin and inclusions. Educational Circular No. 12, University of Nebraska-Lincoln, Conservation and Survey Division, 32 pp.

Partlow, D. P. and A. J. Cohen 1986. Optical studies of biaxial Al-related color centers in smoky quartz. *American Mineralogist* 71: 589-98.

Pewkliang, B., A. Pring, and J. Brugger 2008. The formation of precious opal: Clues from the opalization of bone. *Canadian Mineralogist* 46: 139-49.

Ramsdell, L. S. 1955. The crystallography of "coesite." *American Mineralogist* 40: 975-82.

Robbins, M. 1994. *Fluorescence: Gems and minerals under ultraviolet light,* Phoenix: Geoscience Press.

Roberts, W. L. and G. Rapp, Jr. 1965. *Mineralogy of the Black Hills.* Bulletin No. 18 of the South Dakota School of Mines and Technology, Rapid City, South Dakota.

Rogers, A. F. 1928. Natural history of the silica minerals. *American Mineralogist* 13: 73-92.

Ross, N. L., J.-F. Shu, R. M. Hazen, and T. Gasparik 1990. High-pressure crystal chemistry of stishovite. *American Mineralogist* 75: 739-47.

Rossman, G. R. 1994. Colored varieties of the silica minerals. *Reviews in Mineralogy* 29: 433-67

Sanders, J. V. 1964. Colour of precious opal. *Nature* 204: 1151-53.

Sanders, J. V. 1968. Diffraction of light by opals. *Acta Crystallographica* A24: 427-34.

Sanders, J. V. 1975. Microstructure and crystallinity of gem opals. *American Mineralogist* 60: 749-57.

Sclar, C. B., L. C. Carrison, and C. M. Schwartz 1962. Optical crystallography of coesite. *American Mineralogist* 47, 1292-1302.

Sharp, T. G., A. El Goresy, B. Wopenka, and M. Chen 1991. A post-stishovite SiO$_2$ polymorph in the meteorite Shergotty: Implications for impact events. *Science* 284: 1511-13.

Skinner, B. J. and D. E. Appleman 1963. Melanophlogite: A cubic polymorph of silica. *American Mineralogist* 48: 854-67.

Smith, D. C. 1984. Coesite in clinopyroxene in the Caledonides and its implications for Geodynamics. *Nature* 310: 641-4.

Smith, E. 1999. *Black opal fossils of Lightning Ridge.* East Roseville, NSW: Kangaroo Press, 112 pp.

Smith, F. G. 1958. Transport and deposition of the non-sulphide vein minerals. VI. Quartz. *Canadian Mineralogist* 6: 210-21.

Staebler, G. and G. Neumeier 2007. Ethiopia to Indonesia: a sampling of lesser-known opal localities. *extraLapis English* 10: 76-80.

Strong. L. 1998. Agates from the land of pumas and craters. *Rock & Gem* 28 (12): 80-3.

Tamara, M. and M. R. Preston 2009. A statistical reassessment of the evidence for the racemic distribution of quartz enantiomorphs. *American Mineralogist* 94: 1556-59.

Townsend, J. 2007. Perfect conditions, perfect spheres: opal formation in Australia. *extraLapis English* 10: 18-21.

Tribaudino, M., A. Artoni, C. Mavris, D. Bersani, P. P. Lottici, and D. Belletti 2008. Single-crystal X-ray and Raman investigation on melanophlogite from Varano Marchesi (Parma, Italy). *American Mineralogist* 93: 88-94.

Vasconcelos, P. M., H.-R. Wenk, and G. R. Rossman 1994. The Anahi ametrine mine, Bolivia. *Gems & Gemology* 30 (1): 4-23.

vom Rath, G. 1868. Ueber den Tridymit, eine neue krystallisirte Modification der Kieselsäure. *Annalen der Physik und Chemie* 135: 437-54.

vom Rath, G. 1887. Ueber cristobalit vom Cerro S. Cristóbal bei Pachuca (Mexico). *Neues Jahrbuch für Mineralogie, Geologie und Palaeontologie* 1887: 198-9.

von Lasaulx, A. 1876. Mineralogisch-kristallographische Notizen, VII. Melanophlogit, ein neues Mineral. *Neues Jahrb. Mineral.* 1876: 250-57.

Whitten, D. G. A. and J. V. R. Brooks 1972. *The Penguin dictionary of geology.* London: Penguin Books, Ltd.

Zachariáš, J., V. Žáček, M. Pudilová, and V. Machovič 2005. Fluid inclusions and stable isotope study of quartz-tourmaline veins associated with beryl and emerald mineralization, Kafubu area, Zambia. *Chemical Geology* 223: 136-52.

Žák, L. 1972. A contribution to the crystal chemistry of melanophlogite. *American Mineralogist* 57: 779-96.

Introduction to Radioactive Minerals. Robert J. Lauf. Collectors have long admired uranium and thorium minerals for their brilliant colors, intense ultraviolet fluorescence, and rich variety of habits and associates. Radioactive minerals are also critically important as our source of nuclear energy. Understanding them is crucial to the safe disposal of radioactive waste. This book provides a

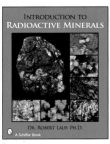

systematic overview of the mineralogy of uranium and thorium, generously illustrated with nearly 200 color photos and electron micrographs of representative specimens. Includes an historical discussion of the discovery of radioactive elements and the development of uranium and thorium ore deposits, a discussion of the geochemical conditions that produce significant deposits, and a description of important localities, their geological setting and history. Major occurrences of interest to mineral collectors are arranged geographically. The minerals are arranged systematically, to emphasize how they fit into chemical groups, and for each group a few minerals are selected to illustrate their formation and general characteristics. With the resurgence of interest in nuclear power, this book is an invaluable guide for mineral collectors as well as nuclear scientists and engineers interested in radioactive deposits.

Size: 8 1/2" x 11"   196 color & b/w photos   144pp.
ISBN: 978-0-7643-2912-8   soft cover $29.95

Collecting Fluorescent Minerals. *Revised & Expanded, 2nd Edition.* Stuart Schneider. Seeing fluorescent minerals up close for the first time is an exciting experience. The colors are so pure and the glow is so seemingly unnatural, that it is hard to believe they are natural rocks. Hundreds of glowing minerals are shown, including Aragonite,

Celestine, Feldspar, Microcline, Picropharmacolite, Quartz, Spinel, Smithsonite, plus many more. But don't let the hard-to-pronounce names keep you away. Over 850 beautiful color photographs illustrate how fluorescent minerals look under the UV light and in daylight, making this an invaluable field guide. Included are values, a comprehensive resources section, plus helpful advice on caring for, collecting, and displaying minerals. The field of collecting fluorescent minerals is relatively new and this is one of the most complete references available.

Size: 8 1/2" x 11"   870 color photos   192pp.
ISBN: 978-0-7643-3619-5   soft cover $29.99

The World of Fluorescent Minerals. Stuart Schneider. The rich and diverse world of fluorescent minerals is explored in this sweeping survey. Breathtakingly pure colors, with their ethereal glow, immediately capture your attention. Did you know that color television is a result of the study of fluorescing minerals? Fresh finds of fluorescent minerals are showing up regularly around the globe,

and their collection is an entertaining and popular pasttime. To help the collector, over 825 photos display the minerals both as they might be found in daylight and in under the effects of ultraviolet light. Written for the collector and the merely curious, this pictorial reference will enrich your collecting experience with its informative text. It is an essential source for enjoying and identifying fluorescent minerals.

Size: 8 1/2" x 11"   825 color photos   176pp.
ISBN: 0-7643-2544-2   soft cover $29.95

Schiffer books may be ordered from your local bookstore, or they may be ordered directly from the publisher by writing to:

Schiffer Publishing, Ltd.
4880 Lower Valley Rd.
Atglen, PA 19310
(610) 593-1777; Fax (610) 593-2002
E-mail: Info@schifferbooks.com

Please visit our web site catalog at *www.schifferbooks.com* or write for a free catalog. Please include $5.00 for shipping and handling for the first two books and $2.00 for each additional book. Full-price orders over $150 are shipped free in the U.S.

Printed in China